Considerate Con

ISBN print: 9781326817664; ebook: 9781326817657

Published in the United Kingdom by
Content Design London
Kemp House, 152 City Road,
London EC1V 2NX

Copyright © Content Design London

First edition published March 2025

Original design Mark Hurrell, revised design by Catherine Lutman

Rebekah Barry has asserted her right under the Copyright, Designs and Patents Act, 1988, to be identified as Author of this work

All rights reserved. No part of this publication may be reproduced or transmitted in any form or by any means, electronic or mechanical, including photocopying, recording, or any information storage or retrieval system, without prior permission in writing from the publishers

Content Design London does not have any control over, or responsibility for, any third-party websites referred to or in this book. All internet addresses given in this book were correct at the time of going to press. The author and publisher regret any inconvenience caused if addresses have changed or sites have ceased to exist, but can accept no responsibility for any such changes

A catalogue record for this book is available from the British Library

This book is typeset using GT America

Printed by Lulu.com

hello@contentdesign.london
www.contentdesign.london

Considerate Content

How to make your content more inclusive and accessible, with a focus on neurodivergence and health conditions

Rebekah Barry

**Content
Design London**

Contents

Foreword		6
Introduction		9
Part 1	Context and definitions	18
Chapter 1	Understanding the language we use	21
Chapter 2	The models of disability	25
Part 2	Practical advice on how to make digital content more inclusive and accessible for everyone	32
Chapter 3	Clear language	35
Chapter 4	Structure and style	55
Chapter 5	Images	73
Chapter 6	Video and audio	89
Chapter 7	Using emojis	99

Part 3	How different conditions can affect how people experience content	**106**
Chapter 8	Neurodiversity	**111**
Chapter 9	Bipolar disorder and depression	**145**
Chapter 10	Aphasia	**159**
Chapter 11	Deafblindness	**175**
Workshop	Naming things	**189**
Conclusion		**203**
Further reading, references, and attributions		**207**
A note about research		**212**
About the author		**213**
I appreciate you		**214**

Foreword

You may think this book is for content designers. And it is. However, it will also help literally anybody who writes anything with the expectation that other people will read it. Whether you're an interaction designer, a content creator, a policy maker, or an educator, this book serves as a guide for making your content more inclusive.

Accessibility is a hot topic, and rightfully so.

With each new generation of people, society's views on disability are changing. The knowledge around disability and inclusion is growing, and standards and regulations are adapting rapidly to accommodate it.

Pretty much everybody in product design is talking about colour contrasts, the Web Content Accessibility Guidelines, and making things 'compliant'. But, ironically, what people rarely talk about is how to actually write content that is accessible.

You might be wondering, how can you build a product that is accessibility compliant, but has inaccessible content? It sounds paradoxical, right? But this is a problem with a lot of the 'compliant' products we see today. There's a fundamental issue with how people adhere to the Web Content Accessibility Guidelines. Almost all of the content design guidance is categorised as level AAA, and therefore it's not covered by any legislation. So, everybody inevitably just ignores it.

You can have a product that uses complex academic language, which is full of jargon, acronyms, and metaphors that nobody can understand. But as long as a screen reader reads it aloud and the accessibility checker says it's fine, everyone pats themselves on the back, marks it as compliant, and ships it. This is the world we live in.

Foreword

Digital services are only getting bigger, more complex, and more seamlessly woven into our everyday lives. Over the past 20 years, they have replaced the way we do education, banking, commerce, and even how we socialise. So the need for accessible content has never been more important.

The significance and timing of this book cannot be understated. From start to finish, it's filled with good intentions, real-world experiences, and solid, practical advice. It addresses a crucial gap left by our endless fixation on accessibility compliance, and it aims to improve our collective understanding of what it truly means for content to be accessible.

The future of accessible content is not just in the hands of content designers, but in the collective will of any of us who create, share, and consume it. This book is a step towards that future. A literal playbook for those who aspire to make content clear and usable. I challenge anybody to walk away from reading this book without feeling more informed, empathetic, empowered, and equipped to make practical changes to their own work.

Reflecting on my own journey, I feel both honoured and well-positioned to write this foreword. As an autistic with ADHD, who often relies on the guidance outlined in this book, but also as a digital accessibility specialist, and the former Head of Accessibility at the Department for Work and Pensions, where I first worked with Rebekah.

For as long as I've known Rebekah, she has consistently been at the top of her game, and this book is no exception. So, I'd like to take this opportunity to say: thank you for all that you do, in pushing the agenda, holding people accountable, and for just making the world a bit easier for people like me.

Craig Abbott

Introduction

I have always been motivated by social justice. When I trained in law, my specialism was working with people who needed legal aid. I then went into the charity sector to help people who needed advice when they were in difficult or vulnerable situations.

In 2014, I got a job as a content designer at Citizens Advice, the UK's largest advice-providing charity. Citizens Advice were setting up a user-centred design team, and they were (and still are) committed to creating content that helps people. I worked with user researchers for the first time, and the user-centred focus meant my work was prioritised by what the most people needed help with. That turned out to be content about benefits for people with ill health and disabilities.

As content people know, you can't create great content without doing research.

The researchers I worked with were consistently phenomenal. Having worked in the advice sector for such a long time, I thought there was no story or circumstance I hadn't heard. I was spectacularly wrong.

We spoke to a lot of people. They shared their experiences of what it was like to live with a disability or health condition. More often, they lived with a combination of conditions. They didn't just share what it was like to try to get help from a website. They also shared what their everyday life was like.

The research meant we created content that worked for people with wide-ranging needs, at a hugely stressful time in their lives.

Trying to get the money you're entitled to from the government is no mean feat. This brings me to my next move.

From Citizens Advice I moved to the Department for Work and Pensions, the part of the UK government that decides people's welfare benefits. I worked on disability assessments. You may have heard about these assessments as they were often the subject of news stories, most of them not good. I was in the room for a number of them.

These assessments were often insensitive and, in some cases, heartbreaking. People had to focus on their worst days and bring forward the hardest aspects of their lives to get the money they needed. Most had complex, intersectional needs: our bodies affecting our minds, our minds affecting our bodies, and our physical and emotional environments affecting both.

What people say, and the insights they give, stick with you. Years later I still think about some of the people who allowed me to observe their assessments.

The research I've been involved in has not just affected but defined my content work. I've been lucky and privileged to hear people talk about their lives and share their insights. Unfortunately, many of us producing digital content don't work in teams and organisations that can give us the time and resources to gather these insights.

On some projects, the research participants bring such great understanding into the content work, and teach you so much about a particular aspect, that the whole team talks about them. These participants are often those with needs that hadn't been considered. These are the insights we tell our stakeholders about and that make the most significant difference to our websites, products, and services. These insights, which often seem like small details of the participants' own lives, make us remember the important lessons that their experience taught us. Being told what to do to improve content is very different to understanding why, and the real life context makes you remember.

The experiences that people have shared over the years has given me the knowledge I'm going to share in this book.

I want to give you a taste of that real-life experience, particularly if you're not working in an environment that allows you to hear these insights for yourself.

For me, accessibility and inclusion are about social justice. They are intertwined and interrelated, and they motivate my work. As you'll learn throughout this book, accessibility and inclusion are not just tick boxes on a compliance chart. Being considerate of people's wide-ranging needs is central to making things better for everyone. That's what considerate content means and does.

What you'll find in this book

Part 1 gives context and definitions of the language and phrases used throughout the book.

Part 2 gives practical advice to make digital content more inclusive and accessible for everyone, including people with any of the conditions we focus on in Part 3.

In Part 3, you can read stories of people with different experiences and needs and consider why and how you can create better content for them.

Things you won't find in this book (that you might be expecting)

All the answers
This book gives guidance and examples of what works and doesn't work for some people, and the reasoning behind why things do or don't work for them. It isn't possible to give a definitive set of rules for how to make your content inclusive and accessible for everyone, as there isn't always a correct answer for all audiences. There is, however, plenty of guidance for you to apply that will improve your content for everyone.

The best way to see if your content works for the people using it is to talk to them about it. This gives you insights into what works for them and how you can improve it. You will never reach the point where it works for everyone, but you can try to make it work for as many as possible. This book helps you to do that.

How to meet the Web Content Accessibility Guidelines (WCAG) international standard
The Web Content Accessibility Guidelines are a set of international standards developed by the World Wide Web Consortium (W3C) and used around the world. The standards consider the experience of people with cognitive or physical impairments or disabilities who use assistive technology or access websites in non-conventional ways.

I spoke to fellow content people about the Web Content Accessibility Guidelines whilst researching this book. Some people thought that I should cover the guidelines and what is expected of you as content creators. After a lot of thought, I decided not to cover the guidelines.

Let me explain why.

Even if I went through every expectation for meeting the AAA standard, I could not advocate that it was enough. If a website achieves level AAA, by the Web Content Accessibility Guidelines measures it is a fully accessible website. It gives the impression of being a high bar, but in reality, the content recommendations at this level are still inadequate. This is why I've chosen not to go through the standards individually.

As an example, let's look at guideline 3.1.4, which covers abbreviations. To comply at level AAA, you must have 'a mechanism for identifying the expanded form or meaning of the abbreviation available'.

Firstly let's recognise that the quote in the previous sentence was tough to understand. I'll translate. It means that the abbreviation has to be written out in full somewhere. Examples are given in the guidelines of where it might be found (or, let's be honest, hidden) in a 'tooltip' or a glossary.

I would recommend that, in most cases, you should give an acronym or abbreviation in full every time you use it.

There are many reasons why, such as:

- by only giving the full form only once, you expect people to remember an unfamiliar concept later on, which can be hard,
- referring to a glossary is distracting, time-consuming, and not a great experience,
- people using screen magnifiers may have difficulty going back and finding the previous mention of the abbreviation where it is given in full because they are looking at a much smaller portion of the screen,

- showing the full version of an acronym or abbreviation in a tooltip as suggested will not work for lots of people. Tooltips can be distracting for people who have problems with their attention and can be challenging for people with limited sight or limited dexterity.

To comply at level AAA, you just need to ensure people can look up the acronym or abbreviation. This isn't good enough. I didn't want to write a book about how to do the bare minimum to meet standards. Instead, I'm aiming for something genuinely helpful.

Another reason I don't go through all the criteria to meet the Web Content Accessibility Guidelines is that content people all have such different responsibilities. Some of us might be the sole content designer, responsible for many aspects of design. Others might work with designers or developers who have responsibility for things like colour contrast, images, and coding. So it's difficult to decide the criteria we might potentially need to cover.

While it isn't my intention to give a guide on how to comply with the Web Content Accessibility Guidelines at a certain level, nothing recommended in this book will fall short of the current AAA standard.

The law
I wrote a very long chapter about the law in various jurisdictions and why it's important. Then I threw it away.

Most legislation says that websites must meet the AA standard of the Web Content Accessibility Guidelines. The guidelines related to content are all at AAA level, a higher standard seen as just recommendations or best practices. So issues with content are extremely unlikely to win you a legal case.

Some people will use the threat of legal action as a way of trying to make organisations have clearer content. In reality, that's not going to happen. Yes, thankfully, there are laws to protect against the discrimination of disabled people in most jurisdictions. But these laws cannot make an organisation change the way it writes.

Part 1
Context and definitions

1
Understanding the language we use

The World Health Organisation estimated that about 16% of the world's population is disabled, which is around 1.3 billion of us.

In the United Kingdom, the Department for Work and Pensions estimates that about 16 million of us are currently disabled. That's nearly 1 in 4 of the population. 45% of adults over pension age and a majority of people over 80 self-report as disabled. ('Self-reporting' means they describe themselves as having a disability.)

In the United States, census data shows that about 42.5 million of the population are disabled. That is about 13%. Other estimates are much higher, with the Centers for Disease Control and Prevention estimating that around 27% of adults in the United States are disabled. This is about 1 in 4, so it correlates with the United Kingdom.

That's a lot of us, and that's only really considering people who may have accessibility needs.

When we think about inclusion and who is historically and systemically excluded because of, for example, their gender, race, sexuality, age or economic status, we are talking about most people. When you combine all of those systemically excluded groups, accessibility and inclusion is a majority issue.

In this chapter I cover some important concepts. The aim isn't to give a perfect definition, but to explain what I understand them to mean in the context that I have used them. You may have different ideas about what things mean to you, and that is all good.

Accessibility and inclusion

The Cambridge Dictionary defines accessibility as 'the quality of being able to be entered or used by everyone, including people who have a disability'. The same dictionary defines inclusion as 'the act of allowing many different types of people to do something and treating them fairly and equally'.

I think the definition of accessibility is okay, but I don't align with the definition of inclusion. The word 'allowing' within the definition of inclusion feels the opposite of inclusive as it indicates a power dynamic. Who, in this definition, has the power to 'allow' another person to do something?

The concept of treating people 'fairly' is also problematic here. Who says it's fair? This indicates another power dynamic. Treating people 'equally' is not working for me either as equality is about giving people the same thing and assuming that's fair. Equality doesn't take into account people's different needs and circumstances. The term 'equity' is about recognising those differences in needs and circumstances and allocating what's needed to ensure an equal outcome. Inclusion should be more about equity than equality.

These dictionary definitions sum up why definitions can be difficult and inadequate, so I will talk about it a little rather than trying to define things precisely.

What I mean by accessibility and inclusion

Accessibility and inclusion are related, but they are not the same.

In the context of websites and digital products, accessibility means ensuring that the product or service is designed and developed to be usable by everyone, including those with disabilities or other needs, regardless of their abilities or the tech they are using. Accessibility is a fundamental principle of design that supports equity and inclusion but does not create equity and inclusion in itself.

Inclusion is a broader concept that encompasses more than just access. Inclusion ensures that everyone, of any identity or background, feels welcome, valued, and respected.

Everyone should experience websites, digital products, and services in a way that is respectful, dignified, and considerate.

If accessibility makes sure you can get in, inclusion should then make you feel welcome.

2
The models of disability

The academic discipline of disability studies looks at and devises theories of disability and creates models around those theories. The models aim to help society develop strategies and policies to meet the needs of disabled people.

There are many models of disability, but the 2 main ones that people refer to are the medical and social models.

You might wonder what this has to do with content, but the models influence how we talk about disability and each other.

The medical model

The medical model of disability comes from the point of view that a person has a medical impairment that disables them and excludes them from aspects of society. The aim is for the impairment to be 'fixed' so that a person is no longer disabled and excluded because of it. The medical model inherently sees an impairment or difference as a bad thing that should be eliminated if possible.

Thinking the way of the medical model can lead to exclusion and segregation. For example, the medical model approach might assume that a child can't go to their local school because of the level of help they need, and then provide a separate school for children needing extra help or equipment.

The social model

The social model of disability comes from the perspective that a person has a difference and that society is disabling and excluding them by its design and attitudes.

For example, you might use a wheelchair and be unable to get into a shop. In the medical model, you can't get into the shop because you can't walk unaided. The emphasis is on you.

In the social model, you can't get in because the shop has a big step and a narrow doorway. It has been designed in a way that disables you.

Designing the entrance to the shop differently would mean you can access it without problems and would not exclude you from shopping there.

Designing that shop without a step and wider doors would also help a whole group of people who don't use a wheelchair. For example, it would help:

- blind people not trip up or down a step,
- parents with a buggy,
- trying to squeeze through with a lot of bags.

The list is endless. The no-step and wider door design would not exclude anyone who had no trouble using the poorly designed shop entrance.

I've given a highly simplified explanation. Of course, not all impairments can be negated through design and attitudes, but everyone should be able to live a decent quality of life no matter what impairments they have.

Person-first or identity-first language?

We talk about disabilities in 2 ways: person-first and identity-first. This is a sensitive issue, and it's best to be clear and up-front that there is no 'correct' answer about which to use in all cases.

Person-first language is when you put the person first and the identity second, so 'a person with a disability'. Examples of person-first are 'Anna has autism' and 'people with hearing impairments'.

Person-first language reflects the medical model of disability that a person 'has' something that disables them. People outside of disabled communities often use person-first language as they think it sounds more polite and that they're not defining a person by their disability. Doing this assumes that the condition is disabling them and is intrinsically 'bad'.

Identity-first language is the opposite. You say the identity as part of the person's being, rather than something they 'have'. So identity-first would be 'a disabled person' rather than 'a person with a disability'. An example of identity-first language is 'Anna is autistic' rather than 'Anna has autism'. Although in this example her name comes before her condition, it is identity-first because it shows autism as part of her being, and not something she 'has' and that is secondary.

Identity-first language reflects the social model of disability. A person is who they are, and their environment and society decides whether to disable them or not.

Person-first language would sound bizarre if you consider other characteristics like gender, race, and religion. For example, I am white. I don't have whiteness. She is Jewish. She doesn't have Judaism.

Some groups are fighting for an identity-first approach. From my own experience, many autistic people firmly believe that their autism is an intrinsic part of who they are and that should be respected. That's not to say that there aren't some autistic people who prefer to say that they have autism.

Most communities of disabled people and groups advocating for disabled people use identity-first language. This is not to say that people who use person-first language about themselves are wrong. People have a right to use whatever language they want about themselves.

Sometimes people who have become disabled during their life use person-first language. This can be because they know themselves without being disabled, so their essence of themselves does not involve their disability. For example, all the people I spoke to said they 'had aphasia' and did not say they were aphasic. Aphasia is a communication impairment that I will focus on in chapter 10.

Some conditions are so defined by the medical model that it's hard to use identity-first. For example, ADHD is Attention Deficit Hyperactivity Disorder. As it has been labelled a 'disorder', it makes it harder to say 'I am ADHD'. The people I spoke to said either that they 'have ADHD' or referred to it as 'my ADHD'. This differs from neurodiversity, which is about how our brains work differently and sits very much in the social model. It would be unusual to hear someone say that they 'have' neurodivergence. Instead, they say they're neurodivergent.

There isn't a correct answer about which to use. People have their own preferences. The general advice is just ask, but that only really works on an individual level. You're bound to have some people using your content who prefer person-first and some who prefer identity-first.

When you're creating content about disability or health conditions, speak to your audiences to understand what their preferences are. This means you can make an informed decision on whether you use person-first or identity-first language. You can also give the rationale in the content itself for why you chose that term, so your audience understands your reasoning even if they personally disagree.

I have mainly used identity-first language in this book unless the people I interviewed spoke about themselves in person-first language. I decided to reflect the social model over the medical model of disability.

Part 2
Practical advice on how to make digital content more inclusive and accessible for everyone

This section has practical advice on what to think about when creating digital content. This covers general accessibility recommendations that make content better for everyone, while Part 3 covers recommendations for specific conditions.

Sometimes advice might contradict other advice. This is because people have different needs, but there are plenty of aspects that improve things for everyone.

This part covers:

- clear language,
- structure and styling,
- images,
- audio and video,
- using emojis.

3
Clear language

Making our writing complicated is a habit that we learn at an early age. When I left school, I went on to do A levels and had to write essays that had an all-important word count.

There must be students who think, 'I have 2,000 words. If I write clearly and concisely, then I can fit in a lot more points and get a great mark'. Unfortunately, I was not one of those students. So 2,000 words was a finish line that I would drag myself to an hour before the deadline by filling the essay with all kinds of waffle and pointlessness.

There was also the marvel that was the thesaurus. Why use a simple word when there are so many exciting words that barely get used and, most importantly, will make me look clever? My giant red hardback thesaurus got a lot more use than my dictionary, as looking clever was the priority, not being clever.

Then came the job applications. It seemed impossible to say, 'I did x'. So instead, I used 'I had responsibility for' and 'obtained extensive knowledge of', even when the limits of my extensive knowledge and experience were stacking shelves. I thought I must look 'professional', which meant sounding nothing like my authentic self.

After escaping the confines of shelf-stacking, I got a holiday job working for a recruitment firm. One of my duties was to polish resumes, or CVs, depending on where you're from. By polishing, I mean making them sound impressive. It seemed most people looking for a job had got the memo about making their employment history as complicated as possible, but there were always bigger words I could add. I'd worry about whether I'd used professional terms like 'Yours sincerely' or 'Yours faithfully' correctly when sending letters off to potential employers.

As we enter the adult world, we have already learned some horrible writing habits.

It's hard to unlearn this conditioning, and that's the battle when using clear language.

It's pretty challenging to make something simple. Creating clear content is a craft that takes skill. But once you learn to let go of the habit of making things complicated, it's hugely satisfying to keep simplifying until the content is down to its essence.

Plain language and plain English

Although they are often used interchangeably, plain language and plain English aren't the same.

The term 'plain English' is often associated with the Plain English Campaign, which is a commercial enterprise. Plain English doesn't involve testing the content with readers. It is a series of techniques to use when writing content; for example, using short sentences and not using specialist language.

Plain language differs from plain English as it involves researching and testing the content. It is plain language if people can understand and act upon it.

The International Plain Language Federation's definition is:

'its wording, structure, and design are so clear that the intended readers can easily find what they need, understand what they find, and use that information'.

An example of the difference is that the readers may be specialists and use jargon as the primary way of talking about something, in which case using that term makes it understandable for them. But if your content is, for example, for people with aphasia, it would need to be different to be understandable.

While there is nothing wrong with the techniques the Plain English Campaign recommends, research and testing are crucial to know if people can understand and act upon your content. There is one thing in particular that I feel is absolutely wrong about the Plain English Campaign's guidance. They say that plain English is quicker to write. Although it might appear to be a minor point, it is revealing. Getting content right for your audience is hard work and often takes a long time.

One of the main problems with using plain language is that, whilst we can all agree it is a good thing, we often underestimate the complexity of our content.

It's hard to see that something isn't easily understandable to others when you understand it yourself. This is why it's so important to test your content.

I've decided to refer to plain language as clear language as the word 'plain' feels negative and has connotations of being boring. Plain language is too special and precious for a negative term. Plain language is a reliable workhorse, but it's also beautiful in its simplicity, so I'm giving it a little brand refresh.

I'll go into more detail on the following aspects of clear language:

- choosing the right words,
- writing in the active voice,
- using pronouns and being reader-centred,
- avoiding acronyms and abbreviations.

Choosing the right words

A big part of making content clear is the actual words you use. I know this sounds obvious, but the problem is that what you think of as clear words is highly subjective. You can't just rely on your judgement, or you could end up replicating your own vocabulary, which could be totally different to that of your readers.

Here are some more objective ways to choose the right words.

Use everyday words

Using everyday words makes content more usable and less likely to exclude people. If you want people to take action, they need to know what you're saying, and you don't want to slow them down by making them think about what words mean.

On a service I was working on, a Deaf research participant referred to 'junk words'. These are words that are unnecessary or over-complicated and they aren't used in sign language. I love this description. Let's eliminate all the junk words.

As a side note, I mentioned a 'Deaf' participant above. You may see deaf styled in lowercase ('deaf'), capitalised ('Deaf'), or written as 'd/Deaf'. These are different terms used by the community to describe different types of hearing impairment.

- deaf = functionally deaf in the medical sense, but not culturally Deaf, and less likely to communicate using sign language
- Deaf = culturally Deaf and part of the Deaf community, usually communicates in sign language
- d/Deaf = you're talking about or addressing both of these groups of people

People who learn English as an additional language are told that if they know 2,000 to 3,000 words in English, they can cover about 90% of everything they need to know to get by. So we should ensure we use the words people are more likely to know.

Although using a word with a precise meaning can be satisfying, a more common and less precise word is usually fine and will exclude less people. I know some of you think I should have said 'fewer', but 'less' has the same meaning and is a more common word. I understand that using the 'wrong' term can be jarring for some people who feel strongly about using traditional conventions. Still, language evolves, and I feel that understanding is more important.

You can find lists online of the most common words in your language if you want to check and compare words. Have a search online and see what you find. For example, according to one list, 'use' is in the top 50 most commonly used words, and 'utilise' is somewhere around the 80,000 mark. So someone with a basic level of English would understand 'use', but they would need a vast vocabulary to understand 'utilise'.

If there is a word that means the same thing and is more common and more straightforward, use it! (Don't 'utilise' it.)

Avoid Latin

Some Latin is commonly used in English. For example, 'eg'. I had to look up what 'eg' stands for, and I'm never sure where the punctuation goes, even though writing is my job. Using 'for example' is easier for people to understand.

This is the case for most Latin terms; for example, 'ie', which I also had to look up. I wasn't sure of the difference between it and 'eg'.

One of the most common examples of Latin usage is 'status quo', but it wouldn't be difficult to use easier words to describe this concept. Of course, there are exceptions. Some Latin phrases are well understood and used regularly; for example, per cent and its slightly less proper Latin evolution, percent.

Latin is generally problematic for two reasons. First, it's not commonly understood. Second, it can make content come across as a bit pompous and clever. It's alienating.

Some audiences use Latin in their work, like lawyers and doctors. Although most lawyers don't spend their days shouting 'Caveat emptor!' ('Let the buyer beware!'), some Latin terms aren't translated to English when commonly used, like 'ultra vires' ('beyond the powers'). But unless you have an extremely specialist audience, it's better not to use Latin terms unless no alternative is more understandable.

Words that mean 2 things: homographs and heteronyms

English has a lot of homographs, which are words that have the same spelling but more than one meaning. For example, the word 'bat' can mean an animal and also a thing that hits a ball. When the 2 words are spelt the same but pronounced differently, they are also heteronyms. For example, the word 'content' is a heteronym. It is pronounced differently when talking about digital content than when feeling peaceful and content.

Heteronyms can cause problems for screen readers, especially if they don't have enough context to tell the software how to pronounce them. For example, a screen reader might be okay with the sentences 'she was feeling content' or 'let's all try to create the most inclusive digital content' because the sentences around the word 'content' give it context. However, the word 'content' as a label on a dropdown menu or data table might cause problems because there is no context.

It's important to test your content with screen reading and text-to-speech software to check the pronunciation. Although you can't guarantee that all screen readers and text-to-speech software will interpret the words in the same way, it will give you an indication.

Use the same words as your audience

To make content clear and understandable to your audience, you must use the words they use. People can't find the content unless it uses the words they are searching for.

Whilst using the simplest, everyday words will always help, there are instances where you will need to go deeper to understand the vocabulary of your readers.

You should research your audience's words and make sure that you're reflecting them.

Methods for finding the right words

Talking to people will give you some insights. But the vocabulary people use when they talk can differ from what they type into search engines. Listening to calls is helpful but might not work for the same reason. For example, sometimes people know official terms for things but wouldn't use them when talking.

If you're looking for the words people use when they're online, you can do desk research to find your audience's vocabulary.

Google Trends

You can use Google Trends to compare words or phrases, how common they are, and where they're used geographically. It's a helpful tool to help you choose between different options. For example, if you weren't sure whether to use 'single parent' or 'lone parent', you can compare them to see which is more prevalent.

When I compare them on Google Trends, I find that 'single parent' is much more commonly used, and 'lone parent' is in decline. In addition, Google Trends shows that the term 'lone parent' is more common in Scotland than in England, Wales, and Northern Ireland, but still less common than 'single parent'.

You can use Google Trends for free:
https://trends.google.com/trends/

Forums and online communities

Forums and online communities can give insights into how people talk about things and their concerns or issues. For example, if you are writing about childcare and your audience is mainly parents, you could look at sites with forums in the UK like Money Saving Expert or Mumsnet to see how parents are describing things.

Social media is a mine of information when you're looking for the words people use to describe things. Going to where your potential readers are chatting is likely to give you more insight into the language they use than more official websites.

Organisations representing causes or communities

If you're writing about a group of people or a community, it's good to look at the organisations that represent them to research vocabulary. You can get insights from the way they talk about things on their websites and in the resources they provide.

For example, if you are writing about LGBTQI+ people, you could look at the information in the UK from Stonewall or GLAAD. Organisations often provide resources for the media and other professionals to talk about the communities they represent. However, be mindful that there will likely not be one answer. For example, GLAAD has fantastic and extensive resources offering education and guidance on telling LGBTQ people's stories, but they do not intend to represent all LGBTQI+ people.

It's best to look at multiple organisations to check for patterns in case you first stumble upon an outlier.

Write in the active, not passive, voice

The active voice is when the sentence's subject comes first and performs the action (the verb).

The passive voice is when the recipient of the action comes after the verb. The passive voice can make it hard to determine who is performing the action.

If explaining active and passive voice through grammatical rules is confusing (as it is for me), then don't worry; examples are coming up.

Often, content sounds woolly or uncertain because it's in the passive voice. The passive voice is popular in 'professional' types of communications because people think it sounds 'official'. It can take the responsibility away from the organisation or person that the content represents.

For example:

- Passive: 100 redundancies will be made by December.
- Active: The council will make 100 redundancies by December.

In the first example, the redundancies are made by some unknown entity; they are inevitable and are nobody's responsibility. In the second example, the council is taking responsibility for the redundancies, and what's happening is clearer.

The passive voice is a valuable tactic to deflect responsibility, so the reader doesn't know exactly what is going on and why.

Here's another example:

- Passive: The cookie was taken by the child.
- Active: The child took the cookie.

And one more:

- Passive: The race will be swum by 100 participants.
- Active: 100 participants will swim the race.

In these examples, the passive voice can help deflect blame (as in the child taking the cookie). But it also adds more words to the sentence, and it uses complicated constructions like 'will be swum'.

The passive voice creates a gap in understanding that the reader or listener has to fill in for themself. It can be confusing. It's clearer to say who or what the doer is unless it's irrelevant.

Pronouns and centring the reader

A pronoun is a word that replaces a noun. For example, in the sentence 'I have written this book', 'I' is the pronoun that replaces the noun 'Rebekah'.

You should address the reader as 'you' and refer to yourself as 'I' or 'we' as long as it is obvious who 'I' or 'we' are. Writing the name of an organisation, team, or person instead of 'we' or 'I' can be confusing. For example, let's say you are working for a fictional organisation that rehomes pets. Compare these 2 versions of content saying the same thing:

1. Pet Rehomers match people with their ideal pets based on their circumstances.
2. We match you with your ideal pet based on your circumstances.

In the first version, it's not clear that you are, in fact, Pet Rehomers. You are, in effect, creating a third entity that can make the reader think, 'Well, who are you then?' The second version clarifies that you are the rehomers, and the reader wants a pet.

When you're writing content, you will get some indications about whether you're on the right path by how easy it is to address the reader as 'you'. If it feels wrong to say 'you', it might be because you're not targeting the content to a specific audience.

Let's say you're still working for Pet Rehomers, and you need to put content on the website to explain the rehoming process. There could be more than 1 group interested in the process; for example, the people who need to have their pet rehomed and those who want a pet. As it's unlikely that anyone would need to know about both processes, it might be appropriate to have 2 different pieces of content that both use 'you' as they are each targeted to 1 audience.

Abbreviations, jargon and figurative language

Abbreviations

Abbreviations are shortened versions of a word or multiple words. It's usually a catch-all term for shortened words or phrases. There are different types of abbreviations, and people use different words to describe similar things. These include:

- shortenings,
- initialisms,
- acronyms,
- contractions.

Shortening

Shortening is sometimes used as a catch-all term for shortening words or phrases, but there isn't universal agreement on this. Some people use shortening to specifically mean making a word shorter by dropping part of it. For example, a phone is a shortening of a telephone, and a fridge is a shortening of a refrigerator.

Initialisms

Initialisms are when the first letter is taken from a group of words to form another word, or collection of letters. They are usually names of things. For example, in the United Kingdom, the NHS is an initialism of the National Health Service. In the United States, the FBI is an initialism of the Federal Bureau of Investigation. Initialisms are spoken by saying the letters individually.

Acronyms

Acronyms are when an initialism forms a word that is spoken as a word. For example, NASA is an acronym of the National

Aeronautics and Space Administration. People say 'nasa' rather than 'N.A.S.A.'.

It's common for people to refer to all initialisms as acronyms, even though it's technically incorrect.

Contractions

Contractions are when part of a word is removed to make it shorter. For example, 'Dr' is a contraction of 'doctor'.

The word 'contraction' is most commonly used when 2 words are merged into one word with an apostrophe. For example, 'don't' is a contraction of 'do not', and 'you've' is a contraction of 'you have'.

Why you should avoid abbreviations

Most website and digital service content is scattered with abbreviations, especially in large organisations and public bodies.

Organisations love abbreviations, especially acronyms and initialisms. Their people claim to dislike them, but something doesn't add up, as an organisation is its people.

People probably mean that they don't like abbreviations they don't know and don't notice the ones they do know.

If abbreviations are okay if you know them and not okay if you don't, they are exclusive by nature.

Clear language is fundamental to creating content people can understand and act upon, and most abbreviations aren't clear language.

Write it out in full every time
It's common practice to write out acronyms and initialisms in full the first time you use it and then use the shortening. This puts an expectation on the reader to remember it the first time or scroll back and find it again when they encounter it later.

Having to remember or go back and find it takes longer than reading it in full again.

Imagine that you're using a screen magnifier on your phone. How long would it take to go back and find where it was initially referenced, and then go back to where you were? Don't imagine; try it for yourself. It's a real pain.

Some initialisms and acronyms are exceptionally well known or are just words in themselves (for example, taser). Those are often widely understood. But in most other cases, initialisms and acronyms exclude and slow people down.

Figurative language
Figurative language is words and phrases that are not literal. Figurative language is big in song lyrics, poetry, and fiction. But it's not so good in the context of people needing information or wanting to complete a task.

Some common types of figurative language are:

- metaphors,
- similes,
- idioms,
- hyperbole,
- personification.

Metaphors are a way of describing something by saying it is something else. For example, 'you are my sunshine' doesn't mean that a person is a ball of fire radiating at them.

Similes are a way of describing something by saying it is like something else. For example, 'shine bright like a diamond'.

Idioms are sayings that literally don't make sense but have been used so much that a group of people commonly understand them. Examples of idioms are 'over the moon' and 'a storm in a teacup'.

Hyperbole is an extreme exaggeration that is not meant to be taken literally. For example, 'I've seen this film a million times'.

Personification is when you speak of objects or ideas as if they have human qualities; for example, the everyday sentence 'my phone died' or the more poetic 'the grass danced in the breeze'.

Avoiding figurative language

Figurative language is usually exclusive to a group or culture, so it immediately excludes people who are not in that group or familiar with that culture. The most obvious examples are people who use English as an additional language, those who are from a different culture, or both.

There are unlikely to be any situations where the people using a piece of content will all be part of the same cultural group with the same level of understanding of language.

Some autistic people take things literally, so language that doesn't make sense when taken literally might be confusing and slow them down.

Figurative language is unlikely to be understood by everyone, so by using it you are choosing to exclude.

Jargon

Jargon is words or phrases a group uses, usually in a work environment. It's a bit like workplace or professional slang. However, people outside of that environment don't usually understand it. Jargon can be specific to an organisation, industry, or a particular profession, and there is also more generic 'business' or 'corporate' jargon. This is sometimes called 'business speak'.

Organisations and industries often have their own jargon, as do specific professions. For example, if you are working in a digital team for an airline, you might have terminology specific to aviation (for example, 'de-plane', 'ceiling', or 'ETD') and terminology specific to digital ('sprint', 'CMS', or 'ticket'). You may have people in the organisation who don't understand digital jargon and others who don't understand aviation jargon. You can't assume that everyone in an organisation knows the same jargon. They often don't.

I have worked in multiple large organisations with unfamiliar vocabulary, and it can be embarrassing to ask what the same things mean multiple times.

I've often heard that this language is only internal, that 'we' know what it means, and that the public doesn't have to deal with them. This might be the intention, but it's not true. They leak out.

I worked for the Department for Work and Pensions, part of the UK government, where acronyms were endemic. Services that people have no choice but to use to get money for their basic survival include a set of acronym-laden hurdles. I doubt anybody intended for this to happen.

These acronyms don't stay inside organisations. You can Google any government acronym, and millions and millions of results appear. The public has to deal with them every day, essentially having to learn a new language. That's not good enough. People deserve better.

Technical terms

Industries and professions will have technical terms that are indecipherable to those outside of that industry or the industry's customer base, but that doesn't mean they are jargon. For example, in skincare, people will be familiar with the term 'retinoid', a derivative of vitamin A used for anti-ageing products. People with no interest in skincare will not know what it is, but that doesn't make it jargon. It just makes it a technical term. There isn't a more straightforward way of saying retinoid. If you're selling a retinoid, you might want to explain what it is, but your customers will likely not be put off by the term.

Excluding people with language

Not knowing what something means and having to think about it is not just irritating. It can also make people feel bad. 'Should I know that? Am I a bit stupid? They've already said what this is. I don't remember, and I should remember. I don't think this is the place for me'.

Nobody wants some content to make someone feel down on themself or that they don't belong.

Checklist for creating clear language content

Make sure that you:

- [ ] Use everyday words.
- [ ] Avoid Latin.
- [ ] Are careful with words that mean more than one thing.
- [ ] Use the same words as your audience.
- [ ] Write in the active, not passive, voice.
- [ ] Centre the reader (call them 'you').
- [ ] Avoid abbreviations.
- [ ] Avoid figurative language.
- [ ] Avoid jargon (but not technical terms).

4

Structure and style

Over 25 years ago, the Nielsen Norman Group found that 79% of people wanted to scan web pages before reading them. The development of eye-tracking software has confirmed that people scan digital content. They don't read it like they would a book. This is true for both those using their eyes and those using screen readers, who often skip through content.

We visit web pages with a purpose and need to know quickly and easily whether we have come to the right place.

A good page structure is vital to comprehension, particularly for those using a screen reader. Without a decent structure, you will frustrate the people using the page and potentially lose them.

Paying attention to structure is one of the simplest and most effective ways to make content more accessible.

This means thinking about:

- headings and titles,
- sentence and paragraph length,
- how to align text,
- how to order content.

Headings and titles

Page titles

A page title should describe the purpose of the content on the page so the reader can determine whether it meets their needs.

The page title doesn't show on the page itself, but it is likely to be shown in 2 places:

- at the top of the browser window. If you scan your open tabs, the page title will be what's written on the tab.
- the main link in search engine results. The text you click on in the results is usually the page title.

When you're putting content into a content management system (CMS), there might be a field called 'page title' that will appear for you to fill in. It could also be called 'title tag' or 'meta title'.

The page title should help people understand what is on the page and if they want to read it. This is particularly important for those using assistive technologies, as they might use the page titles to navigate through multiple pages or identify a page they want to read. The page title should make sense as a stand-alone page and not rely on you knowing where you are within the website's structure. For example, if you had a page with the title 'Form', that isn't helpful on its own. If the page was titled 'Renew your adult passport form', that gives context and explains what the page is.

Having a descriptive page title will help search engines find and rank your content appropriately. The page title should be concise, as most search engine results will cut off the page title if it's over 60 characters. If you can't describe the purpose of the page concisely, make sure that the most important information is first, so that it's not lost when it's shortened in the results.

Headings

Headings are built-in styles in document software or a content management system (CMS). They can be formatted to change their appearance (for example, making them a larger size or a different font). When you use a heading style, it contains information that screen readers use to determine the structure of the page.

Label headings correctly so that the page's hierarchy is clear to both someone using a screen reader and someone who can see.

Headings should be labelled from H1 to H6 without skipping any levels in the hierarchy. For example, don't skip a heading style and go from H1 to H3 just because H2 looks too big.

This is an example of what heading styles look like. Remember, you can customise them to change their appearance if you need to.

This is a Title

This is a Heading 1 (H1)

This is a Heading 2 (H2)

This is a Heading 3 (H3)

This is a Heading 4 (H4)

You should follow the heading hierarchy without thinking about the appearance of each heading. Use headings instead of increasing the font size or formatting text to look like a heading.

Headings should be specific, meaningful, and describe what is in the content below. This helps people decide if they will read the content that follows it. Headings describing what's coming are particularly important for those using screen reading software. They might navigate through headings, jumping from heading to heading, rather than listen to the whole page of content.

Label the heading styles, and use them in the right order

A problem with some web pages is that the headings look like the proper headings, but they aren't labelled correctly in the code. They're just styled to be bigger than the main body text. This isn't obvious just by looking at a page. This is a problem for those using screen reading software to navigate through the content as the sections won't be separated.

Headings run from H1 to H6, with H1 the first and usually styled to be bigger.

Headings should be labelled with the correct H1, H2, and so forth. Headings need to run in the right order as screen reading software uses them to navigate. You can usually do this in the content management system (CMS).

Use statements, not questions

Writing a statement should make the heading clearer and quicker to understand because you can:

- front-load the sentence with the keyword at the beginning,

- use a statement that is quicker than posing a question,
- give the answer.

For example, if the heading for this section was 'Should headings be statements or questions?':

- the keywords are at the end of the sentence,
- it is longer than using the alternative statement,
- it doesn't give the answer (you would have to read the content for the answer).

Use sentence case, not title case

Sentence case is when you just use a capital letter at the beginning of the first word, like you would in any sentence. Title case is when there is capitalisation throughout the sentence. There isn't a universally recognised rule, but it's usually that all the 'important' words are capitalised and the minor ones, like 'and' and 'the', are in lowercase.

It is easier to read sentence case than title case because capital letters are harder to read when they aren't in their usual context. People read through pattern recognition, so capitalising words that aren't normally capitalised makes content harder to read.

Title case can also cause confusion about whether to read something as a noun. Let's look at an example.

1. We are Investing in People and Developing Skills.
2. We are investing in people and developing skills.

Example 1 could make you wonder if 'People and Developing Skills' is an organisation or department, rather than just a description of an activity.

Sentence and paragraph length

You can solve many problems of inclusivity and accessibility with simple sentences. It makes such a difference to comprehension.

We are better able to understand shorter sentences, and less able to understand long sentences. Research by the American Press Institute concluded that people could understand 100% of sentences that were 8 words long. But once sentences reached 43 words, people could understand them only 10% of the time.

A sentence should stick to one point. Aim to have an average sentence length of about 15 words. This length has been shown to be good for comprehension. Some benefit from much shorter sentences. For example, the Stroke Association guidelines recommend sentences of about 5 words for those with aphasia. Shorter sentences can also help those with learning disabilities.

Break up and re-write longer sentences, and use bullet points for lists if possible. They are easy to scan and break up a block of text.

You should also avoid long paragraphs. Each short paragraph should contain one main point. When paragraphs meander through lots of points, it can be overwhelming. Breaking paragraphs down to one main point gives our brains the space to work through what we've just learned.

Big blocks of text make it harder for everyone to get through, but they are particularly difficult for some people. For example, some dyslexic people can find big blocks of text difficult, and some people with inattentive ADHD (Attention Deficit Hyperactivity Disorder) will be put off reading it.

Put all the important information first

Have you ever looked for a recipe online, and when you got to the page, found a whole rambling blog post about the author's life? You probably had to scroll for ages to find the actual recipe. Annoying, isn't it? This is a frivolous example and for most people would only be a mild inconvenience, but delaying important information can cause people big problems.

Structure your content so the most important information is first. In journalism it's referred to as the 'inverted pyramid'. This means putting what people need to know first, and the more granular details come later. This way, when some people inevitably stop reading, they have all they need to know.

Lots of us just want to find the main information we came for, and go. Others will want to continue to read more detail.

There are some people for whom this is particularly important. For example, some people with ADHD lose attention, make assumptions about what is coming, and stop reading. Some people feel physical pain when reading so don't want to read any more than necessary. We should give people choices about how much detail they want to go into and not assume that anyone will stick with the content until the end.

Break down instructions and procedures into clear steps

Break instructions and procedures down into clear, logical steps. This is easier to follow, sets expectations, and makes it easier to work through without thinking too much or remembering.

The steps need to be broken down in full, even if they seem small. Some people may get confused if they have issues with their working memory, so instructions should be as simple as possible. It's also important to tell people when they don't have to do anything.

A bad example
How to set up a helpline page
Bespoke helpline pages take at least 10 days to be set up, and if they are to include new organisations, strict criteria must be met before an organisation/charity can be listed.

The full list of permanent helplines can be downloaded at Permanent Helplines. These can be set up at short notice, but the more notice that's given if one is required, the better.

To set up a helpline, the Executive Producer or Commissioning Editor should contact Audience Services [email address].

Full information on helplines can be found on the intranet.

A better example
How to add a new helpline to the directory of support for audience members
At our Random Company, we link to helplines that can give support to people for issues covered in our programmes.

To add a new helpline, you need to:

1. Check that the helpline you would like to create doesn't already exist. The full list is available at [link]
2. If the helpline is for an organisation that we don't signpost to at the moment, please check that they meet our criteria. You can check the criteria at [link]

3. If you need the helpline listing urgently in relation to a programme that's due to broadcast in the next week, call Audience Services on [phone number] and we will help you.
4. If your request isn't urgent, <u>complete the request form</u>, and we will aim to add the helpline within about 10 days.

Avoid laying out content in columns

Most websites now use a single column of text for a good reason: it's easier to read. Content set out in columns like a newspaper can cause problems for screen readers and text-to-speech software, and columns are challenging to navigate.

It's harder for some to keep their place in the text as you have to keep tracking down to the following line more frequently. Some people have problems tracking the text, so columns make this issue worse.

If the columns are long, it can be hard to find the top of the next column to continue reading, especially if you're using a magnifier or have increased the text size.

Fonts, font sizes, italics, and underlining

Some fonts are easier to read than others. Fonts like Arial, Helvetica, and Verdana are easier to read as they are structurally simple, making the text less crowded.

Italics are harder to read than standard text for everyone. For some dyslexic people, they can make the text look crowded and run together. Arial italics, in particular, reduce readability for dyslexic people.

Use a 14- to 16-point font. On a website, this means it must be a minimum of 16px. Some people may need it to be bigger than this, so make sure it's possible to increase the size by 200%.

Avoid underlining unless it is a link, as underlining links is a familiar convention. Underlined text that is not a link is confusing, and people will try to click on it.

Avoid using all capitals

Capital letters can be harder to read. This is because the shape of the word is unfamiliar when spelt out with capital letters.

Using all capitals changes the tone of what you're reading.

USING ALL CAPITALS CHANGES THE TONE OF WHAT YOU'RE READING.

Apologies for shouting.

Hyphens and dashes

Using commas and full stops is better than hyphens and dashes. This is for 2 reasons:

- some screen readers don't ignore them and may read out 'em dash' or 'hyphen', which disrupts the flow of information, but screen readers always know what to do with a comma,
- they create unusual spacing in sentences, which can cause visual distress.

You can read more about hyphens, dashes, and evidence about how readable they are in the Readability Guidelines (Content Design London).

Spacing

It's best to use around 1.5 line spacing to give words plenty of room, as crowding makes things harder to read.

How to align text

Text alignment is how the text runs across the page, and how you align text affects how easily people can read it.

The types of alignment are:

- left-aligned,
- right-aligned,
- centred,
- justified.

Left-aligned is easiest to read

Left-aligned text means that each line starts at the same point at the left edge. It results in a straight edge of text down the left border.

You should left align as long as you write in a language that runs left to right, like English. It's easier to read. It's the most natural alignment for the eyes of left-to-right readers, which for most people track back to the same point at the beginning of the following line.

Don't right align text unless it's absolutely obvious why

Right-aligned text means that the end of each line of text is aligned to the right edge. It causes a straight edge of text down the right border.

Unless you're writing in a language that runs right to left, like Arabic or Urdu, you should avoid right alignment. It's unnatural for the eyes of left-to-right readers, as it causes the new line to start in a different place each time.

There are exceptions to this. For example, it is a convention for addresses on the top of letters to be aligned to the right. If there is a component on the right side of the page, then it makes sense for the text to be right-aligned, as long as it's just a short piece of text.

Don't centre paragraph text
Centred text is aligned to the midpoint of the line, creating gaps and sometimes a long space at the left and right borders. It is sometimes used as a design choice, and some think it looks prettier than other alignments. It's popular on social media, with statements and quotes often being centred. Let's say it's the Instagram alignment of choice.

Centred text is harder to read than left-aligned text. At the beginning of every new line, you have to look for where the line starts, which can disrupt the reading flow. Also, it's annoying and unnatural for your eyes.

Centred text can also cause problems for those who magnify their screens. When they zoom in, they can miss some text because it's in the middle of the line and not at the beginning where it's expected to be.

Don't justify text
Justified text is spread across the page to reach both margins, leaving uneven spacing between words and sentences. It's less readable because we read by recognising the patterns of words and sentences, not by reading letters and words in order. The uneven gaps disrupt the patterns your eye is looking for.

The uneven spacing creates distracting whitespace, which can cause visual distress to some people with dyslexia. It can create 'rivers' of white that run down the screen and make reading harder.

The issues caused by justifying text get worse when you increase the text size.

Examples of the same paragraph in different alignments
Here is the opening of 'The Great Gatsby', by F. Scott Fitzgerald, in different alignments.

Left aligned
In my younger and more vulnerable years my father gave me some advice that I've been turning over in my mind ever since.

'Whenever you feel like criticizing anyone,' he told me, 'just remember that all the people in this world haven't had the advantages that you've had.'

Right aligned
In my younger and more vulnerable years my father gave me some advice that I've been turning over in my mind ever since.

'Whenever you feel like criticizing anyone,' he told me, 'just remember that all the people in this world haven't had the advantages that you've had.'

Centred
In my younger and more vulnerable years my father gave me some advice that I've been turning over in my mind ever since.

'Whenever you feel like criticizing anyone,' he told me, 'just remember that all the people in this world haven't had the advantages that you've had.'

Justified

In my younger and more vulnerable years my father gave me some advice that I've been turning over in my mind ever since.

'Whenever you feel like criticizing anyone,' he told me, 'just remember that all the people in this world haven't had the advantages that you've had.'

Checklist for structure and style

Make sure that you:

☐ Give a descriptive page title.

☐ Use descriptive headings and section headings.

☐ Label your headings correctly.

☐ Write the headings as statements.

☐ Write headings in sentence case.

☐ Use sentences that have one point only.

☐ Write an average sentence length of no more than about 15 words.

☐ Have paragraphs that cover one main point only.

- [ ] Put all the important information first.
- [ ] Break down any instructions and procedures into clear steps.
- [ ] Lay out the text in a single column.
- [ ] Use a clear font in size 14 to 16, with no italics or underlining.
- [ ] Don't use all capital letters.
- [ ] Avoid hyphens and dashes where possible.
- [ ] Use 1.5 spacing.
- [ ] Align text to the left.

5
Images

Using the right images can enhance the experience of using a website or app. For example, images can help people understand the context of the information, make a page more visually appealing, and send a message about your brand.

Before you use an image, consider whether it's needed and what function it's serving. Images should serve a purpose and be beneficial.

But as well as thinking about alternatives to images for people who might not be able to see them, it's just as important to think about what your images are saying. Using the right image can make people feel included and 'seen'. Using the wrong image can send a powerful, negative message. Unfortunately, it's all too easy to get images wrong, which can lead to excluding people.

Accessible imagery

Assistive technologies like screen readers can't decipher images, and neither can search engines. So it's vital to add a text description to images so that:

- people using assistive technologies can be included and understand what the image is,
- if the page doesn't load properly or someone is saving data on their mobile device, the text will replace the image,
- search engines can index it so people can find it.

Text alternatives can be given as:

- alternative text (alt-text),
- captions,
- long-form explanations elsewhere on the page or on another page that you link to.

Which option you choose will depend on the type of image you're using.

Alternative text (alt-text)

Alt-text is also sometimes called alt-tags and alt descriptions. It is written text that is usually hidden from view as part of the image's metadata. Alt-text is:

- read by screen readers,
- shown instead of the image if the image doesn't load.

Alt-text is usually a few lines. If you find your alt-text is several paragraphs long you should use a long-form explanation, which is explained later in this chapter.

You will usually add alt-text into a field in your content management system (CMS). The leading social media platforms allow you to add alt-text if you upload an image.

How to write good alt-text

Keep the description short

A good alt-text description is generally a short sentence. Use a proper sentence that describes the image as if you were describing it out loud. The description should be clear and give people using assistive technologies the same experience as those seeing the image.

You don't need to say 'image of' or 'picture of' in your alt-text description. A screen reader will give the reader that information. However, information about the context might be helpful, such as 'close-up' or 'screenshot'.

Don't repeat things

Don't repeat things that are already in the text. For example, your content might be about a vase that costs £35. You might have a sentence that says, 'This porcelain vase costs £35', and then have a picture of the vase. That picture might also have the words '£35' in it.

If you include that in your alt-text, a screen reader would read out:

'This porcelain vase costs £35'.

It would then read the alt-text:

'A blue, round vase that costs £35'.

Don't assume that all people using alt-text are blind or partially sighted

People use assistive technologies for all kinds of reasons. Some people use a screen reader because they have problems using a mouse or are dyslexic.

You can include colours and other descriptive words in your alt-text. While people who have always been blind will not have experience of those colours, other people who use alt-text will. Make sure you consider both audiences when you write your alt-text, though.

Don't fill alt-text with keywords for search engine optimisation (SEO)

Alt-text is read by search engines, whereas images aren't. Alt-text and other text alternatives can be helpful for search engine optimisation (SEO), but they are primarily for people, not search engines. Bad alt-text can be like an over-enthusiastic hashtag fest on social media, which is inconsiderate to the people listening.

Don't use alt-text as an opportunity to make jokes

When the platform then known as Twitter made it more obvious and easier to add alt-text, people started using it as an opportunity to make jokes or say more than they could within the constraints of 280 characters. In this situation, the joke only makes sense for people who can both see the image and read the alt-text. This is not the purpose of alt-text.

Don't make assumptions about the motivations of people in the image

It's important not to add subjectivity to the motivations or emotions of people in the image. Alt-text should factually describe what is happening in the image, not interpret it. Emotions can be trickier as sometimes the purpose of using an image is to show joy, for example. In this case, it would be acceptable to include the emotion in the alt-text; but as a general rule, we shouldn't assume we know how people in images are feeling. For example, you should say that a person is smiling, rather than saying they're happy.

Captions

A caption is text that sits by the image and explains it. The advantage of a caption is that a screen reader and other assistive technologies can read it, and sighted people can also read it.

Captions usually give the context of an image rather than just a description. As captions and alt-text serve different purposes, you should use both.

For example, a news story with a picture of an athlete holding a gold medal might have a caption that says 'Pat Mustermann has won the title of fastest underwater basket weaver in history'. The caption gives context to the image, but doesn't describe it. The alt-text of that image might be 'a close up of Pat Mustermann in a Germany team top, holding up a gold medal near his face in his right hand. He is smiling'. The alt-text adds a description that provides part of the story to someone who can't see the picture.

Long-form explanations

Because alt-text should only be a few short sentences, there might be times when you need a longer explanation of visual content. This is often the case if you use complex images like graphs, maps, or charts that would need a lot of explaining.

Writing long-form explanations for complex images is a challenging task. Before writing the description, you should consider:

- the purpose of the image and what information it is conveying,
- in what order you should explain it,
- how to explain the information objectively, particularly data.

Once you have written your long-form explanation, you will need to decide where to put it. If it is too much for alt-text or a caption, you could put it on the page, making it clear that it is a text alternative. Or, if it is particularly lengthy, you could give it a page of its own and link to it.

Types of images and how to describe them

Images might be:

- informative,
- decorative,
- functional,
- complex.

Informative images

Informative images convey something that you can explain simply. They give another way of looking at what the text is saying.

A simple example might be an image to show where the charger plugs into a phone.

Sometimes it's hard to decide whether an image is informative or purely decorative. For example, a website for single parents might have a picture of a father with a child. You might think this image is decorative, but its purpose might be to convey that male single parents are welcome.

If an image aims to evoke a feeling, it is informative.

How to describe informative images
Informative images need a text alternative so everyone can understand the information. You might choose to use a caption or alt-text.

Decorative images

When you use an image purely to add some visual interest, like textures and patterns, this is a decorative image.

Decorative images don't add meaning to the content. If you take them away, the interpretation would be the same.

How to describe decorative images
Purely decorative images don't need alt-text.

However, some people want to know what is there and feel excluded by not knowing.

Others prefer no alt-text description because it's unnecessary and slows them down when using assistive technologies.

The most common advice is not to include alt-text on decorative images. This means the screen-reader has an instruction to ignore the image, rather than looking for a description to read and not finding one. You can do this by 'setting the alt-text to null'. In practice, that means that in the alt-text field you write "" (2 double quotation marks with no space or text in between them).

Ignoring alt-text on decorative images might be something you want to test if you can do some research on your content.

Functional images

Functional images represent an action. For example, an illustration of a bin means 'move to trash'.

Designing functional images isn't common for most content people unless you are working on a new website or app. However, it's useful to be aware of them and know how to describe them. You can work with your developers to make sure they have been properly described.

How to describe functional images
The purpose of functional images is often to perform an

action. For example, the icon of a printer is to print, so you would put the action in alt-text.

It's important to describe the action and not the icon itself. Consider a warning icon of a red triangle with an exclamation point in it. The icon indicates you're about to lose work that you haven't saved. You would want the alt-text to say 'Warning image. Your work is not saved', rather than 'A red triangle with an exclamation mark in it. Your work is not saved'.

Complex images

If the information in an image is too complicated to explain in a short sentence (like for an informative image), it's a complex image. A complex image could be an infographic, map, diagram, or graph.

How to describe complex images
Complex images can't usually be explained in a short sentence as simple informative images can. This means you probably can't use the usual alt-text to explain them, and you will need to write a long-form explanation.

Images that contain text

As a general rule, don't use images that contain text. Images with text are pervasive on social media, like inspirational quotes on Instagram or screenshots on X (formerly Twitter), for example.

Images that contain text are problematic because:

- they can be hard to read and get fuzzy if you zoom in or use a screen magnifier,
- text over a picture can be hard to read for everyone and especially bad if you are visually impaired,

- screen readers can't read the text in an image,
- you can't customise the text in images, which some people need to do to read it.

There are some legitimate reasons to use images of text, for example:

- logos,
- charts and graphs,
- products that are for sale.

There are also some reasons that are not so legitimate, like it being a workaround because your content management system (CMS) won't let you put text where you want it. This is terrible for accessibility, so don't do it.

Inclusive imagery

My son recently started nursery school. On his first day, I had to fill in a form to permit school to use his image for various things. The list of these things started with a choice: would I allow them to share photos with me on an internal system? The next question: could other parents on that system see the photos? Then it asked about sharing pictures on the school walls, social media, and school brochures.

As soon as I saw this form, it filled me with dread.

I'd only seen white children at the nursery, and my mind immediately skipped to him being front and centre on a school brochure: the curly-haired, mixed race boy as the token face of the school's diversity.

I have no reason to think that the school would do this, but it's such a common occurrence that it was my first thought. We've all seen a corporate website that, for example, uses the same woman wearing a hijab in multiple photos.

We know the importance of using diverse images, but sometimes we don't consider whether the images are inclusive. Diversity without inclusion can be performative, tokenistic, and, at worst, damaging.

Using a diverse range of people in images, and the consequences

Using a diverse mix of people in images is usually cited as a good thing. This could be to:

- reflect the organisation's diversity,
- show that the organisation is committed to inclusion,

- show that the product or service is for everyone,
- attract a demographic you're not currently attracting.

Using the example of the school, they might use my son's image to show they are committed to inclusion and see the school as a welcoming place for everyone. But if they were opportunistic, it could be mainly for the last reason: to attract a demographic they don't currently attract.

Let's say you're a parent looking for a nursery school for your Black child. As well as the anxieties that all parents have about finding childcare, you're worried about exposing your child to racism. If the website has a picture of a Black child on the home page, you don't know the reason behind the school's motivation.

If it's to reflect that there are Black children at the school, then great. The picture might reassure you that your child is less likely to be on the receiving end of racism.

If it's to show that the school is committed to inclusion and welcoming to everyone, the picture might reassure you, depending upon whether the school actually is racially diverse and how worried you are.

If the school is motivated by a need to attract Black families because they have none, it's problematic. There's no reason for you to think this is a safe place for your child. Unless there is a very good reason for the lack of diversity, like it's in a small rural town with only white people, it probably isn't a safe place.

These issues are not just applicable to race.

For example, you might be a woman applying for a job at a majority-male start-up. If there are many images of women on the website, you can get the wrong impression about the culture.

You could be a wheelchair user buying a ticket for an event that has a picture of a wheelchair user on the events page, but no lift at the venue. The examples are endless.

Using 'diverse' images to attract a demographic you aren't currently drawing can potentially damage the people you hope to attract, no matter how good your intentions are. It might be uncomfortable to realise, but it's trickery.

Be authentic in the images you present so that people can make their decisions based on the truth.

How to choose representative and inclusive images

The first rule is to be truthful and authentic. You can be thoughtful and considerate when choosing images, but they're a mistake if they don't represent the truth.

Portray people positively and with agency

A starting point is to think, 'would I be happy with that image if it was of me or someone I loved?'

Portray people positively and with agency. Nobody wants to be seen as a victim or someone who needs help. Unfortunately this does happen, particularly to disabled people and people in lower socioeconomic groups. So if there's the slightest inkling that an image might be condescending or negative, don't use it.

Think beyond skin colour

Skin colour is often assumed to be the easiest way to show diversity of people because it's harder to see things like sexuality and most disabilities. This is why there is often a problematic over-reliance on using an inauthentic spectrum of skin colour to express inclusion.

There are other ways to include and represent all people, some more subtle and some that people tend to forget.

Include people of all genders by not relying on standard stock photos of people. They tend to be very masculine or feminine. Instead, use real people of all genders. Using a diverse range of real people, you can include more than just cis male and cis female.

Although sexuality is not something you can see, relationships and families are. You can include people of all genders in relationships with each other and all different types of families.

Age and body type are sometimes overlooked. Both are easy to show visually. Attractiveness is subjective, but images tend to show people that comply with a particular western standard of beauty. This is also an easy one to improve on.

Think about subtle cues that show people that those like them are welcome. This could include clothing and headwear, badges, and things on the walls.

Don't stereotype, use cliches, or misidentify people
This is an area where the difference between diversity and inclusion shows itself. It can also reveal your biases.

In 2019, a research report by Adobe found that two-thirds of African-Americans and over half of Latino and Hispanic Americans felt that their ethnicity was stereotyped in adverts.

Avoid stereotypes. For example, a university website may, on the surface, show a diverse group of people. But if it portrays Black students playing basketball and Asian students in a maths lecture, it's stereotypical and offensive.

There are some cliches to avoid, such as photos of different-coloured hands and 'diverse' people high-fiving each other on a sports field. Also, beware of showing disabled people as 'inspirational' instead of just folk getting on with their business.

Don't misidentify anyone. If you are using an image of a group of people, make sure your caption and alt-text accurately describe what is happening. For example, don't take a photo of a group of women at work and use it to show a 'women in tech event' if that's not what was happening.

Also consider whether showing an image of people could compromise them in any way; for example, identifying their protected characteristic or a certain condition when they possibly haven't shared that information publicly.

Use diverse and inclusive stock photo websites
If you need to use stock imagery, use a website specifically for diverse and inclusive images. There are lots of them, and they're easy to find.

6
Video and audio

Text alone can exclude many people for lots of reasons. These might include having low vision, limited literacy, or using English as an additional language.

Providing a video or audio as well as text gives more people access to the content and a choice over how they receive information or enjoy the content.

A video or audio file might be:

- the primary content; for example, a podcast,
- an alternative format to text content,
- there to help people understand the text content.

Videos

First things first: here are a lot of ways that video content can exclude people. Creating videos is a significant investment of time and money that you should consider carefully to avoid common problems.

Video content can be distracting and overstimulating for some, and flashing images can lead to epileptic seizures. You can read more in-depth evidence about the advantages and disadvantages of using videos in the Readability Guidelines (see Further reading, references, and attributions).

If you do decide to use video, here are some things to keep in mind.

Don't let videos autoplay

Sometimes videos will start to play automatically on a website or app without you interacting with it. This is called 'autoplay'.

Videos that autoplay are horrible for many reasons. If you're using a screen reader and a video starts playing, it can interfere with the content you were trying to listen to.

If you're using a screen magnifier, it can be hard to find where the video is on screen and how to shut it down.

Autoplay can be distracting for some autistic people and some people with ADHD.

Lots of people are deeply irritated by auto-playing videos. It's often a scramble for the 'x' to get rid of it as quickly as possible.

Instead, make sure any video can be started, stopped, and controlled by the person watching it.

Captions and subtitles

Subtitles and captions both involve adding words to a video to reflect what is being said. However, they are not the same.

There is helpful advice online about writing subtitles and captions, particularly from the UK charity Scope.

Captions
Captions are a text version of spoken dialogue and other audio elements that are not speech, such as an alarm going off or a dog barking.

Good captions don't just transcribe what is said. They may also give additional information, like saying if there are important background noises. Captions also indicate who is speaking.

For example:
Caroline: I'm going to be late!
[fire alarm sounds]
Michelle: Now you are going to be even later! [laughs]

Captions are essential to understand what's happening in the soundtrack if you can't hear it, and they are also helpful when you just don't want to listen to something out loud. Some people find it helpful to both hear and see the words to help them understand the content.

Pre-recorded videos with sound need captions.

It's best not to rely on the auto-captions provided by some platforms (such as YouTube) as they're not always accurate.

Closed and open captions

Closed captions are often called subtitles in the UK, although they are not technically subtitles. You can turn them on or off, and their functionality depends on the media player you use.

Open captions permanently appear in the video, and you can't choose to turn them off. They are not dependent on the functionality of the media player you're using.

> **"**
> Videos that aren't captioned and are automatically played can be a real challenge – and annoying for everyone.
>
> Molly (Molly is deafblind).
> **"**

Subtitles

Subtitles are words on the screen that reflect, or translate, the spoken words in the video. They are primarily used by people who don't understand the language being spoken. Subtitles used in a film assume that the audience can hear but not understand what is being said.

In the UK, we often use the term subtitles for both closed captions and translations.

Transcripts and audio description

Videos should have both:

- a text transcript to describe what happens in the video,
- an audio description that you can play while watching the video.

A text transcript lets people who can't hear a video with sound read the audio content. People who use a screen reader can either listen to it or, if they have the assistive technology and are braille users, convert it and read it that way. You must ensure that the transcript is accessible for screen readers and text-to-speech.

A transcript also means that search engines can index the content covered in the video.

Audio description

Audio description describes what is happening in a video, beyond the words and noises. It will include visual clues and elements that aren't conveyed by sound or audio.

For example, a video might show a piece of paper swirling in the wind around an empty classroom. A caption might say:

[sound of wind blowing]

A subtitle would say nothing, as there are no words being spoken.

Audio description might say:

[A gust of wind rattles through an empty classroom and blows a single sheet of paper around the desks.]

This can be helpful for, among others, people with cognitive or learning disabilities, those with aphasia, and people who are blind or partially sighted.

If the video has sound, the audio descriptions should convey what's happening in the video during the natural pauses.

> **❝**
>
> If you have a video on a website, some caption it but don't offer a transcript. Some people who are deafblind need a transcript. If you're captioning your videos, why not have a transcript as well? Both do a good job.
>
> Molly (Molly is deafblind).
>
> **❞**

Sign language

Some people with sign language as their first language might benefit from a sign language video.

British Sign Language is one of many sign languages. It's important to know that it is not English translated into signs, but a distinct language. People who communicate using sign language may not be fluent in the language of their country, so we can't assume that a deaf person can read English. For that reason, some sign language users might find it hard to process a transcript or captions on a video.

Audio

Audio-only content is rare on websites, but there are lots of apps that have audio-only content. Common types of audio-only content are podcasts and audiobooks.

If you are creating audio content for any platform, here are some things to consider.

Eliminate background noise

Be mindful of any background music or noise. Many people will have problems hearing the main content if anything is happening in the background.

Paying attention to background noise won't just benefit those who are hard of hearing. Some people have sensory sensitivities and can't tune out background noise. Make the main content the main focus and eliminate distractions.

Create a transcript

If you are using audio, there needs to be a transcript. Otherwise, you are excluding everyone who can't hear it.

You can use online (or offline) services to create transcripts for you. You should always check these for accuracy. Make sure you put the transcript somewhere logical, easy to find, and in an accessible format.

Podcasts

I'm going to have a rant about podcasts for a minute. Podcasts and audiobooks are growing massively in popularity. The Ofcom Podcast Survey (March 2023) found that about 25% of us in the UK listen to a podcast every week. In the United States the figure is even higher, as podcasts are more established.

The text alternative to an audiobook is, of course, a book. But the text alternative to a podcast is largely nonexistent. Very few podcasts have transcripts. There are rarely transcripts available on the podcast platforms, and often your only hope is that the podcast creator has put a transcript on their own website.

I will give you a highly unscientific example. I listen to a lot of podcasts, and there are a handful that I listen to every week. They are well known, and listening figures are very high, in the tens of millions. But unfortunately I can't find a transcript for most of them. This is a disgrace. It's unimaginable that television wouldn't have subtitles available, and it's the same thing.

There are now more transcripts available than a year ago, when I couldn't find any for the podcasts I regularly listen to. I hope this is a sign of things to come and that podcast creators are becoming more aware that they are excluding people if they don't provide a transcript.

Rant over. If you produce a podcast, please provide a transcript. If you like podcasts and your favourites don't provide a transcript, tell them!

7
Using emojis

A significant majority of people who are online use emojis every day in their personal communications. People love them. They are joyful and fun and brighten up your messages and social media posts. What's not to love?

There are many positives to using emojis for communications and marketing. Studies show they can make brands more attractive, increase engagement, and make people feel happy.

However, I am not convinced that emojis have a strong use case in most content.

Emojis are subjective and up for interpretation by the reader or listener. There are a lot of things that can trip you up and make emoji use inaccessible and exclusive.

Emojis and emoticons

Fun fact: the word emoji does not derive from anything to do with emotions. Instead, it comes from the Japanese: e ('picture') + moji ('letter, character'). In other words, they are pictographs.

Emoticons are representations of facial expressions made from punctuation marks, letters and numbers. They are older than emojis and are related to emotions. The word comes from 'emotion' + 'icon'.

Using emojis

Use emojis, not emoticons
Emojis have alt-text contained in them. That means that screen readers read out emojis in a standard, descriptive way. It may not be the description you would give it or think it is, but it is automatic as it's in the alt-text.

You should look up the description of an emoji before using it, as some of them are a bit random or unexpected.

Emoticons are punctuation, letters, and numbers, and they don't translate into what you are trying to depict. Depending on the screen reading software, a smiley face :-) might be read out as 'colon, hyphen, right parenthesis', or it might be ignored completely. Screen readers often ignore punctuation because we don't say punctuation when we speak.

Don't use emojis to replace words
Replacing words with an emoji makes the content hard to read for everyone. You have to think about what the emoji is or means and then put it back into context.

That is, if you recognise it. Often people don't immediately recognise an emoji or interpret it differently, making the content confusing.

Don't repeat emojis or use a lot of them
A few years ago, a meme was doing the rounds on Twitter. It mentioned 'red flag' behaviour, and then many red flag emojis fill the rest of the tweet.

The biggest red flag about this meme was that many people aren't aware of how inaccessible it is. If you read this tweet with a screen reader (VoiceOver, for example), you would hear the emoji as 'triangular flag on post'. You would hear 'triangular flag on post' about 20 times, but no mention of a red flag. It's very annoying.

Be considerate of people listening to emojis. Hearing repeated emojis can sound like something's broken, and it's time-consuming and irritating.

Use popular emojis that work on all devices
There is some data available on the most frequently used emojis in different regions. It's best to use the ones people use most often to limit the chances of confusion. This can differ by demographic, so you can look into that if you have a very specific audience.

Emojis don't look the same on all devices. Check on unicode.org to see what emojis look like on different devices and operating systems.

Yellow people emojis are not racially neutral
Emojis of people and their body parts used to be yellow. In 2015 changes were introduced to let you modify the skin colour of the emoji to 1 of 5 skin tones, based on the Fitzpatrick Phototype Scale.

Twitter data shows that people with darker skin tones are more likely to change their emoji from yellow to nearer their own skin colour than people with lighter skin tones are.

A 2021 study has shown that people think yellow people are white people. This makes sense when you consider that people often think of them as 'Simpsons' characters, and the Simpsons are pretty obviously a white American family.

The study also looked at people's perceptions of the authorship of the content based on the skin tone of the emoji used. People did think that the emoji represented the author, so yellow equals a white author.

Think carefully before using emojis of people and body parts, as people will associate the colour with the skin colour of the author. If there is not an obvious author, then the skin colour represents your organisation. Unless your organisation represents a specific ethnic group, it's probably best to avoid using these emojis.

Use emojis that are visible in light and dark mode

Most emojis are designed for light mode, and problems can occur in dark mode. For example, a black heart is almost invisible in dark mode.

Check your content in both light and dark modes to make sure it's clear. You can do this by switching between light and dark mode on your phone.

Put emojis at the end of a sentence and after a call to action

Make sure that emojis don't get in the way of important information or an action that a person needs to take.

An emoji looks small visually, but listening to its description can get in the way of reaching an action.

For screen reader users, an emoji mid-sentence can make it hard to understand a sentence as it breaks the flow. Also, someone might stop listening before the important part because they've come to expect emojis to signal the end of a sentence.

Be careful of using emojis to express emotions
Facial expression emojis aren't universally understood as conveying the same emotion.

For example, it was recently reported that some younger people perceive a smiley face as passive-aggressive. Some people might use a winking face to signal a joke or sarcasm. But others might take it as a flirtation, which could be creepy in a professional communication or publication.

Some people struggle to read emotions from facial expressions. The translation of a facial expression into an emoji can be confusing for everyone, as they are often far from obvious, but are particularly difficult for those who struggle to read faces. It means that emojis have become another language to learn, and who needs that?

> **"**
> I have no idea what all the different facial expression emojis are about. It's a smile or a laughing face with tears streaming, then I know it is laughing, rather than a straight face with a tear – that's sad. But there are some of them that I have no idea what they mean.
>
> Naomi (Naomi is autistic).
> **"**

Outside of personal communications, it's better just to make the emotion you're expressing clear in the text.

Part 3

How different conditions can affect how people experience content

In this section, I'll cover some conditions that affect how people experience content. I've divided these into:

- neurodiversity,
- bipolar disorders and depression,
- aphasia,
- deafblindness.

These are not representative of all accessibility issues, but they give a range of things to consider when trying to create content that is more inclusive and accessible.

Each section includes the experiences of people with those conditions, and tips for creating content that works for them.

Symptom soup

In this section, I talk to different people about their experiences and conditions. Many of these conditions involve tangible things that you can observe and that are clearly related to their diagnosis (for example, deafblindness). But other conditions involve symptoms and experiences that are harder to label and are less clear-cut. This is particularly true for neurodivergent people.

It became clear to me when I was meeting people and speaking to them that rarely do people have One Thing. Someone might have a diagnosis of ADHD, but they experience symptoms in their lives that may (or may not) be related to something else. Often these symptoms cross over, or share characteristics, with other conditions. Sometimes they don't.

I would speak to someone about their X and in the course of our conversation they would also talk about their Y and Z. Everyone I spoke to who is neurodivergent had more than one 'thing'. These symptoms and behaviours are wrapped together in their lives. I call it 'symptom soup' because you can't separate the ingredients. They are all together and blended into their experience.

When I present the case studies, you will find that the experiences people talk about are wide-ranging. I was tempted to focus just on the single issue that they are 'meant' to be describing: their experience of dyslexia or autism, for example. But I quickly realised that life isn't that organised. So I have left their experiences and stories as they are. Sometimes you will hear people say 'I'm not sure if this symptom is because of this; it may be this'. As content creators, it doesn't matter. As I said at the start, I'm not trying to write a checklist for a certain condition and how to make content better for that. This is about making things better for everyone.

Real voices

The case studies in this section have been edited down from long conversations, but they are all their own words. I haven't changed the way people speak, or replaced words to standardise the language. It's important to hear people as their authentic selves. I didn't want to show people's lives and experiences as textbook case studies, so there may be words or references that you're not familiar with, just as you would experience if you were in the conversation.

8
Neurodiversity

Neurodiversity means that everyone's brains work in different ways.

The term 'neurodivergent' is used to describe people whose brains work slightly differently. The term 'neurotypical' is used to describe the way a majority of people's brains work.

There are positives to thinking differently, and neurodivergent people have strengths and weaknesses just like neurotypical people.

Many conditions fall under the umbrella term of neurodivergence.

There is no universally agreed-upon list of conditions, but some of the most common ones are:

- Attention Deficit Hyperactivity Disorder (ADHD),
- autism,
- dyslexia,
- dyscalculia,
- dyspraxia,
- dysgraphia,
- Tourette's syndrome.

Many behaviours overlap across the conditions, and many people have more than 1 condition.

Psychologist Nancy Doyle estimated that around 15 to 20% of us are neurodivergent.

It's common for neurodivergent people to also have issues with their mental health, such as depression and anxiety. This is understandable, because our society is built for neurotypical people. But it is still common for neurodivergence to be misdiagnosed as mental illness. This becomes clear as you read the stories of the people I spoke to that are included in this book.

I am going to cover 3 types of neurodivergence:

- Attention Deficit Hyperactivity Disorder (ADHD),
- dyslexia,
- autism.

The 3 conditions covered lead us to a handful of techniques you can use to create better content for neurodivergent people.

ADHD (Attention Deficit Hyperactivity Disorder)

I generally say not to use acronyms and abbreviations, but I make an exception for ADHD. This is because ADHD is more commonly used than Attention Deficit Hyperactivity Disorder. It also avoids saying the word 'disorder', which sounds stigmatising and medicalising.

ADHD can manifest through people:

- having difficulty concentrating (especially on things they don't find interesting),
- experiencing hyperactivity,
- acting impulsively.

The National Institute of Health and Care Excellence estimates that between 3 to 4% of UK adults have ADHD. Worldwide prevalence of ADHD is thought to be about 5%, with the United States being much higher, at about 8 to 10%. It's becoming more common for adults to recognise their ADHD traits and seek a diagnosis in adulthood.

It is commonly understood that there are 3 subtypes:

- inattentive,
- hyperactive or impulsive,
- combined.

A 2017 academic study estimated that about three-quarters of people with ADHD have another condition, known as comorbidity.

Another 2013 study estimated that between 25 and 40% of people with ADHD are also dyslexic, and about two-thirds experience some autistic spectrum traits.

How ADHD affects people's lives

The effects of ADHD are generally more subtle in adults than in children. It's common for inattention to remain while hyperactive traits may ease with age. ADHD is also seen less in women and girls. I am deliberately using the word 'seen' as there is evidence to suggest that women and girls 'mask' their ADHD more and are less likely to be diagnosed as a consequence.

People who are the inattentive type may not have hyperactive or impulsive traits, and the hyperactive or impulsive type may not have inattentive traits. The combined type may have traits of all of these. Everyone is different and can have any combination of traits that affect them differently.

There are also common positive traits that ADHD can bring out, like being:

- creative,
- resilient,
- great at communicating,
- high energy,
- spontaneous.

Inattention

There is a common misconception that people who are of the inattentive or combined type can't focus on anything. This isn't true. The inattention often presents itself when people are doing things they have to do, rather than things they want to do.

When doing things that are not compelling, people who are the inattentive or combined type can find that their attention wanders. They can be easily distracted and might be forgetful. It can be hard to pay attention to details and a challenge to organise and complete tasks and activities. It can be difficult to focus and pay attention for prolonged periods of time, leading to zoning out.

Some people find it hard to stay motivated and see things through, and some may procrastinate or underestimate how long things take. Some people are extremely motivated by something, get really into it and passionate about it, but then lose interest fast.

Hyperactivity and impulsiveness

Physical hyperactivity can be a bit of a stereotype of people with ADHD. Not everyone with the hyperactive or impulsive type will be physically hyperactive. Some people will have traits around their impulsiveness only.

People whose ADHD does manifest physically may have problems sitting still. They may need to fidget and move around to concentrate. It can be hard for them to do things slowly, and they may end up doing a lot of things at the same time.

Impulsiveness can show itself by:

- getting bored and needing excitement,
- taking risks,
- being spontaneous, which may stray into recklessness.

Some people are very talkative and might interrupt or say things that aren't appropriate.

Sometimes hyperactivity can be seen physically. But it can also be internal. It can be hard to cope with stress and frustration, and people may have an inner restlessness, get easily agitated, and be impatient. Some people who experience mental hyperactivity find it isn't obvious to other people, but it can be exhausting.

Hyperfocus

Many people with ADHD experience hyperfocus, a state of intense concentration on something interesting and enjoyable. You could describe it as 'flow', where someone is fully immersed in an activity and everything else is tuned out. People in a hyper-focused state can produce a huge amount in timeframes that might seem ridiculous to other people.

Paul

Paul discovered that he has ADHD as an adult, but he thinks he's probably had it for his whole life.

Like many people with ADHD, he has other conditions, known as comorbidities. He has depression, anxiety, and imposter syndrome, and he gets migraines.

Paul isn't representative of all people with ADHD. These are his own experiences.

> My brain deals with things in different ways, depending on context.
>
> I get distracted by external things. If other things are going on, it will pull my attention away. I get distracted by notifications going off, which immediately pull my attention away.
>
> I need to give my hands something to do to enable concentration, but sometimes the fidget becomes the task, and I lose the thing I'm supposed to be concentrating on. I often need to get up and walk around. I have mechanisms in place to help me focus. I use music, and specific rhythms enable concentration and don't distract me.
>
> I translate things into my own colloquial language and interpret it. This has led to problems, like when I translated a technical phrase into my own words and told my accountant about it. I gave the accountant an answer based on those words, which were wrong, and I got into trouble with payments.

My brain links several things together that may be incorrect because I'm not careful when I'm reading.
I get antsy when there is too much information, or it meanders and doesn't get to the point. I can have total concentration on things I want to do right now and can have a laser focus to get it done. I'm best dealing with the problem in front of me and work better dealing with things in the moment.

If I'm going to find content I need, I'm often excited by finding it, so it isn't a chore. I don't go online to browse. I always want to find something.

I read the beginning and then trick myself into thinking that I've read it all and make a conclusion. I get easily bored and twitchy. I form an opinion or conclusion early and skip to the end. I have to try and think in slow motion to try and not form a conclusion too early.

I can't deal with cluttered websites with small fonts and dense text. I assume the language is complicated and indecipherable, even though it may not be. My brain will say I can't understand it.

I need things to be spaced out, and I can follow instructions all day long. My brain is oddly logical as well as chaotic.

I can usually do things like online services when I've planned to do it and want it done. I might abandon it if it gets too convoluted or circular, but that's frustrating as when I want something done, I want it done. If something is annoyingly complex or hard to use, it will play on my mind that I need to get it done, and I can't concentrate on other things.

"

How to create better content for people with ADHD

Give an outline

It's helpful to give an outline so that people know what is coming and everything is covered upfront. There's more on how to do this in chapter 4.

Put the important information first

Putting the important information first can help someone who might miss something further down if they:

- become distracted before that point,
- assume that they have all the information they need and leave.

Putting the important information first also means that people can see if they're in the right place for what they need, and can leave quickly if they're not.

There's more about this in 'Put all the important information first' in chapter 4.

Clear, concise sentences

Some people can be overwhelmed with too much information and lose interest quickly if the content doesn't get to the point. Sticking to 1 point per sentence makes the content easier to understand.

There's more about this in 'Sentence and paragraph length' in chapter 4.

Use clear language

Use words that people frequently use. Give explanations for new or complicated words so people don't assume a different meaning.

There's more on this in 'Clear language' in chapter 3.

Clear steps and instructions

Break instructions and procedures down into clear steps. This is easier to follow, sets expectations, and makes it easier to work through without thinking too much or remembering.

There's more on this in 'Break down instructions and procedures into clear steps' in chapter 4.

Reminders and placement within services

It's easier to stick to a task if you know how much more you have to do. So it's helpful to know where you are in a process or service and be reminded of what you have done and still need to do.

For processes or services that you can't do in one go or that have an offline element, make sure that people can receive notifications when they have to do something. Don't expect people to remember.

Don't expect people to remember things

People often don't remember things that aren't in front of them. This might be a task someone has to complete, or a concept that has been explained. This applies to acronyms and abbreviations, which should be given in full each time.

Avoid all unnecessary visual distraction

Make sure that there aren't visual distractions on screen that can pull attention away from what someone wants to do or understand. This could be design elements like moving content, unnecessary imagery, or complicated fonts.

This could also include links within the text that can lead people away from what they were trying to do. It's better to put links at the end of the content when people can make a more informed decision about whether they want to go there.

Dyslexia

The British Dyslexia Association estimate about 1 in 10 people in the UK are dyslexic.

Dyslexia mainly affects reading and writing. Dyslexic people are likely to have difficulties with reading and writing.

They might also have problems with their memory, organisation, and vision. They can have issues processing and remembering the information they see and hear.

Dyslexic people are all affected in different ways. It is a continuum, with some people only mildly affected, and others having profound difficulties.

For many people, being dyslexic also brings lots of positives, like being creative, highly motivated, and great at solving problems.

How dyslexia affects people's lives

The difficulties that people experience can be exacerbated by their environment or what they're doing. A dyslexic person can have good days and bad days.

Reading
Reading can be difficult and slow, and it's usually the main problem dyslexic people have with digital content.

Dyslexic people may have problems with comprehension. They often find it difficult to get the meaning of the information from scanning or skim-reading. When reading, they:

- may not recognise familiar words,
- might miss words,

- may add or substitute words.

It's common to mix up words that look similar.

It's common for a dyslexic person to lose their thread and have to reread sentences or paragraphs to understand them.

It can be challenging to track the words accurately. This can be improved or made worse by particular fonts and colour combinations.

Some common content formats can create visual discomfort. These include:

- using big chunks of text,
- italics and capitals,
- crowded content,
- unusual spacing.

It's common to experience glare from reading black text on a white background. This can make it harder to read, and many people use screen tints to bring the glare down.

Writing
Dyslexic people can have problems with writing, particularly spelling. For example, it is common to use letters in the wrong order and to mix up letters that are similar when reversed, like b and d.

When someone is interacting with digital content, writing is less of an issue than reading. Still, there are instances where it can cause problems; for example, using search and filling in forms.

Memory, organisation difficulties, and overload

Dyslexic people can have difficulty holding and retrieving information in their memory. They can also have problems with organisation.

Some dyslexic people get mentally overloaded with too much information. It can be confusing to be given too many instructions at the same time.

Strengths

Although there are challenges, dyslexia can also bring strengths.

Dyslexic people are often:

- creative,
- great at visualising things,
- problem solvers,
- lateral thinkers,
- skilled strategists who are able to see the big picture,
- good verbal communicators,
- highly motivated and persistent.

Jane

Jane is dyslexic, autistic, and has depression. It is common for neurodivergent people to struggle with their mental health, and it is also common for neurodivergence to be mistaken for a mental health issue.

As you will see from Jane's story, it can be impossible to say whether a particular trait is because of autism, dyslexia, or depression. It's common for neurodivergent people to be diagnosed with multiple conditions.

Jane isn't representative of all dyslexic people. These are her own experiences.

> **"**
>
> I was diagnosed with dyslexia when I was in my early 40s. I'd always had my suspicions. It was causing me eye strain, headaches, and exhaustion.
>
> In terms of dyslexia, I have achieved well, and it hasn't held me back, but I struggle with things a lot more. I just don't give up. I developed coping strategies when I was younger, so I always thought it was normal.
>
> I'm very sensitive to sound. If someone is tapping, I feel like someone's trying to drill a hole in my skull. It's almost painful, and it just makes me want to scream.
>
> My communication style is very functional.
>
> If I were reading something aloud to you that I have not seen before, it would be almost like a 5-year-old was reading it. It wouldn't merge into a flow; it would be very staccato and broken up.

I read sentences 3 times. First, I look at every word and read each one as an individual word. Then, I put it together in the sentence, but I still don't have a mental view of what that sentence means. So then I put it together and start to get the meaning out of it.

When I was in an English lesson in school, the teacher said, 'Can you read the next bit out?' I just looked at them and said, 'I don't know what this section means yet, as I've only read the words so far.' I thought everyone read everything 3 times. It was possibly one of the worst things anyone could do. They laughed at me, and it's always stuck in my mind.

I struggled to learn to write, but I don't think dyslexia was really known or widely diagnosed then.

Doing intense, technical reading when you need to understand and follow it is very hard, especially on the screen. It takes a lot of brainpower to process.

Websites in panels or columns are tricky because screen readers don't always get that and sometimes try to read straight across. If there's a picture with text around it, they don't get along well with that either.

I use Texthelp on the computer. I've been using Texthelp for years, since before I knew I was dyslexic. I use the screen reader fairly frequently. I use it for intense stuff, have big chunks of text, or things that need to be right.

I follow along with the screen reader, and the one I use highlights the word that it's on.

I can't listen to audiobooks as I'm very auditory-sensitive. I know how things sound in my head when I read them, and it annoys me when they put the emphasis where I wouldn't put emphasis.

The screen reader doesn't put any emphasis or intonation. It's a very mechanical voice. That's helpful because you can hear the punctuation. It's very obvious whether there's a comma or full stop by the length of the gaps. I like the mechanical voice. I like the very specific timings for different types of punctuation.

You can configure the voice that you use. You can also configure the speed, pitch, and whether it reads out the punctuation.

I think it's probably more to do with my autism than my dyslexia. I can't cope with the emotion, and I get quite annoyed with it.

I'll tint the screen because that helps with reading. The purple screen tint helps with my dyslexia. Without it, the words jumble around. It looks like things are moving, and it's difficult to find when you are on the line. From my perspective, it looks like the words move, but I suspect that my eyes don't stay at the same place on the screen. I might jump down the line that I'm reading or see words duplicated. The high contrast of black writing on a white background is part of the problem. That comes down a lot with the coloured tints and coloured overlays. It makes it much easier to follow where you are in the sentence and keep track of which bits you're reading.

> The screen tint applies to the entire screen. It's just like putting a virtual screen cover over it. Sometimes it makes links and pictures difficult to see. The BBC website is very good for links because they are a more bold type. Whereas some websites have the links in coloured boxes, and that's difficult to see with the screen tint. Anything that already has a blue or purple background becomes too dark to read.
>
> I do struggle with pulling my thoughts between metaphorical and literal. I have more of an understanding when people are talking because of their non-verbal communication. But I do still sometimes struggle with things.
>
> Working out the intention behind what's written is hard, especially with fictional things and working out what the characters mean. I know how it's intended with something like the news, but it is a problem with fiction.
>
> ”

How to create better content for dyslexic people

Many of the problems that dyslexic people encounter with digital content can be improved with some consideration.

We can improve the experience of dyslexic people by thinking about how we:

- use structure and styling,
- write,
- support written content with visuals ,
- provide alternative formats.

Structure and styling

Using clear headings and having a clear structure makes content visibly clear. This is also helpful if someone uses a screen reader as it makes it easier for them to navigate.

It's best to use around 1.5 line spacing to give the words plenty of room, as crowding makes things harder to read.

Don't justify text or use double spacing
You should align text to the left. The uneven spacing of justified text creates distracting white space, which can cause visual distress. Justified text and double spacing can create 'rivers' of white that run down the screen and make reading harder.

Don't lay out content in columns
Content in columns like a newspaper is harder to read and causes problems for people using screen readers and text-to-speech software. They are challenging to navigate.

It can be hard for a dyslexic person to keep their place in the text with the content in columns as they need to keep tracking down to the following line more frequently. Some people have problems tracking the text, so columns exacerbate this issue.

There's more about this in 'Avoid laying out content in columns' in chapter 4.

Use bold for emphasis
The British Dyslexia Association advises using bold for emphasis, rather than underlining or italics. They advise that Arial italics in particular reduce readability for dyslexic people. Underlining and italics can make the text look crowded and run together.

Fonts
Use a 14- to 16-point font, or a minimum of 16px, for websites. Some people may need it to be bigger than this, so make sure it's possible to increase the size by 200%.

Use a sans serif font like Arial, Helvetica, or Verdana. Sans serif fonts don't have the decorative flourishes of serif fonts. They are easier to read as they are structurally simpler, making the text less crowded.

There's more on fonts in 'Fonts, font sizes, italics, and underlining' in chapter 4.

Your writing

Using some basic techniques when writing content, you can significantly improve readability.

Avoid hyphens and dashes
It's better to use commas and full stops instead of hyphens and dashes. This can help someone with dyslexia who might use a screen reader. Screen readers can sometimes read out these types of punctuation, saying 'em dash' or 'hyphen', which disrupts the flow of information.

They can also create unusual spacing, which can make it harder for someone with dyslexia to follow the sentence.

There's more on this in 'Hyphens and dashes' in chapter 4.

Minimise use of capital letters
Capital letters can be harder to read. This is because of the unfamiliarity of the shape of the word when spelt with capital letters. You can still use capital letters for titles and names, but avoid writing whole sentences in capitals or using more than you need to.

Don't use double negatives
Some people may miss words when reading sentences. If you use a double negative, a missed word might make the reader understand the opposite of what is meant. It's also an extra cognitive load to work out the meaning and reverse it. So let's just say it's bad manners.

Avoid acronyms and abbreviations
Capital letters are harder to read, and dyslexic people may see the letters jumbled, so the acronym could become meaningless.

Some dyslexic people have trouble holding information in their working memory, so if you have to use acronyms or abbreviations, write them out in full each time so that you don't expect people to remember.

There's more about this in 'Acronyms' in chapter 3.

Avoid big blocks of text
Big blocks of text can cause visual discomfort and are hard to read. Keep paragraphs short, and use bullets and lists to break up the text where possible.

Use short, simple sentences in the active voice.

There's more about this in 'Sentence and paragraph length' in chapter 4 and 'Write in the active, not passive, voice' in chapter 3.

Give clear and direct instructions
Instructions need to be broken down and clear, even if the steps seem small. Some people may get confused if they have issues with their working memory, so instructions must be as simple as possible.

For example, instead of saying 'Make sure you activate your ticket before you board the bus', you could say:

1. Buy a ticket from the machine at the bus stop.
2. Put your ticket into the machine at the bus stop that says 'Validate tickets here'. You will hear a beep when your ticket has been validated.
3. When you get onto the bus, show your ticket to the driver.

Don't rely on words alone
Words on their own can be challenging, and many people who have difficulty processing the words won't use a screen reader or text-to-speech software.

You can use images and graphics to give context and support understanding if someone finds it difficult to understand the text.

When giving instructions or explaining procedures, it can be helpful to use flowcharts or other visual representations as well as using text. This can help people who understand things more easily when it's visual.

Alternative formats

Consider providing the information in alternative formats like audio and video. Not everyone who has challenges with reading will use a screen reader or text-to-speech software, so providing an audio format might be helpful. Some people can get a better understanding from watching a video than reading or just listening.

Any alternative formats you provide need to be fully accessible. You should, for example, provide captions on videos and alt-text on pictures. More information can be found in chapters 5 and 6.

Autism

Autism affects how a person experiences the world around them and how they communicate. Autism is sometimes referred to as a spectrum condition or autism spectrum disorder (ASD).

All autistic people are different but may share some common characteristics. Autism affects people in different ways, and the spectrum is not linear.

Some autistic people live independently and have developed strategies to live in a society made for neurotypical people, but others have more significant challenges.

Learning disability charity Mencap estimates that around half of autistic people may also have a learning disability.

The National Autistic Society estimates that there are approximately 700,000 autistic adults in the UK.

How autism affects people's lives

The characteristics of autism are different for each person, but the main areas of difference are:

- social interaction and imagination,
- social communication,
- sensory differences,
- repetitive or ritualistic behaviour.

Social interaction, imagination, and communication

Autistic people may have difficulties with social interaction, social imagination, and social communication.

Socialising and social interactions can be difficult and tiring due to their unwritten and changeable rules. Having to read people consciously is hard work, especially when everyone's rules on social interactions are a bit different. This makes it hard to understand what people really mean, making exchanges tricky.

Social imagination refers to imagining what other people are thinking, doing, or feeling. Differences in social imagination can make it hard to understand abstract concepts, hypotheticals, and things that only exist in the imagination. For example, it could be hard to contribute to a conversation speculating how a footballer would have felt if he had been signed by a different club, or if you could only eat one food for the rest of your life, what it would be.

Differences in social imagination should never be confused with a lack of imagination or creativity.

Some people may have difficulties imagining what might happen next if other people are involved, so differences in social imagination also relate to craving routine and repetition.

Differences in social communication can manifest in problems interpreting both spoken language and body language. Processing all that information can be overwhelming. For example, some people take things literally. They find it hard to detect sarcasm or whether someone is joking or being serious.

Sensory differences
It can be challenging for autistic people to process sensory information.

This affects people in 2 ways:

- over-sensitivity or under-sensitivity to any of the individual senses,
- sensory overload.

Having sensory differences can really affect someone's life because it can affect their emotions, especially when things become overwhelming.

Sensitivity to individual senses

A person may be sensitive to light, sound, taste, touch, or have issues with their balance or sense of their own body.

The 2 senses most relevant to experiencing digital content are sight and sound.

People can be over-sensitive or under-sensitive to sight and sound. Over-sensitivity in particular can mean that environments that are too bright or too loud can be overwhelming and irritating.

Examples of light under-sensitivity are:

- things appearing dark or without features,
- having poor depth perception,
- central vision appearing different from peripheral vision.

Over-sensitivity to light can lead to distorted vision, fragmented images, and finding bright lights startling.

People under-sensitive to sound might not hear certain things or only hear in 1 ear, for example.

Over-sensitivity to sound can mean noise is louder than other people perceive, and people experiencing this might not be able to block out background noise.

Sensory overload

When someone finds it difficult to process too much sensory stimulation or information, it can lead to overload. Being overwhelmed can make someone feel stressed and anxious. Meltdowns are when someone becomes physically unable to control their behaviour. Meltdowns can be exhausting for those experiencing them. Shutdowns can mean closing off entirely and are also hugely debilitating.

Repetitive and restrictive behaviour and intense interests

Some autistic people like to have a routine in their lives as it brings some predictability to an unpredictable neurotypical world. Routines can relieve anxiety. Examples of routines could be things like eating a particular food at a set time or taking the same route on journeys.

Some autistic people make repeated physical movements or noises called 'stimming'. Stimming can be enjoyable. It can help someone process what's going on with their senses, or relieve their anxiety, but it can be misinterpreted as being in distress.

It's common for autistic people to have intense interests. However, having narrow and deep interests has many benefits and is not just about relieving stress; these interests bring joy.

Naomi

Naomi is autistic and has mental health issues. She also has difficulties with her hands that affect her fine motor skills, so she sometimes uses assistive technology to avoid using a mouse.

> I was given an autistic spectrum disorder diagnosis when I was 39 or 40, which explained a lot.
>
> I was referred to a psychiatrist for mental health difficulties. He said that I needed to get back to socialising and enjoying people's company again. But I'd never enjoyed that, and it led to an assessment.
>
> I know myself now. I know what I need to do to look after my mental health, and I make myself do it. It's not the same as what works for everyone else, so I don't compare myself to other people.
>
> I loved the Covid-19 lockdown. I loved being at home, not travelling to work and being surrounded by people. When I stopped doing that, I realised how wearing that was and how difficult I found it was. How exhausted I was at the end of the working day. I used to make myself do that.
>
> Constantly engaging with people throughout the day depletes my energy. I did it, but it left me with nothing left, so I'd come home and go to bed at 7pm. It was a much easier world for me... I used to play a role for the day, and I didn't have to act a role at home.

My hands don't work particularly well. They get sore, and I drop things. Sometimes it's just easier not to rely on their precision. My fine motor skills aren't great. Sometimes, I use voice activation, so I don't have to type if I'm out and about or if my hands are sore.

I have learned that I can take things literally. I don't necessarily recognise the joke. I will read things and take it as it is. I tend to have to go back and think, 'Hold on a minute. Is that what they really meant? Or have I taken it too seriously or too literally?'.

I usually recognise metaphors as what they are. Sometimes if I'm asked hypothetical questions, I think I wouldn't do that. I can't enter into the imagination.

It's less of a problem when I'm reading rather than listening or watching videos because there are more clues on the page. Often, there are more clues in the text as to whether it's humour or not. But when I'm listening, I often take it too seriously. I don't realise that it's not as I hear it.

That's what makes human interaction so exhausting. I'll be being earnest, and everyone else isn't. I'll also sometimes think that people are joking, and they're not. I can't tell the difference.

I taught myself how to recognise emotions. I used to do dreadfully. You can learn a lot. I'm learning about reading faces, although I still can't read them. I'm learning about what feeling somebody might have in a situation. I'll ask if it's appropriate.

When I'm reading, I'm looking for all the information. I do rely on language that's very specifically describing the emotion. How am I supposed to know if it's not written down?

Emojis are like another set of rules. Another language to learn. But they can be quite useful. Having an emoji at the end of the sentence can tell me whether it's a joke or not. Once I'm aware of what social conventions suggest a certain emoji means, it can help me decode something.

I have no idea what all the different facial expression emojis are about. It's a smile or a laughing face with tears streaming, then I know it is laughing, rather than a straight face with a tear – that's sad. But there are some of them that I have no idea what they mean.

Sometimes I'll hover over the emoji, so it explains what it means, and that's quite helpful.

I tend to hover over icons and see what they say. And then I'll try them out and see if it does what I want it to do. So I accept that I don't know what they mean.

I get frustrated with things being unclear and think, are you telling me this because you want me to do something? What do you want me to do?

If you can't be clear, I can't be bothered. So I'm not going to read that, or I'm not going to go there.

Anything that seems persuasive rather than factual puts me off as well. I go for information or do a task,

> not to be entertained. If I'm looking for a new provider of something, or a product that I need to buy, I want to see the statistics. I need all the facts about it. I'll skip over the flowery stuff. I make the decisions myself from the information available. I don't need you to tell me that it's this or that. And actually, I don't trust who you are to tell me.
>
> I always pay attention to sources, and I don't get my information from anywhere that I don't consider a trustworthy source. I would prefer the facts rather than the sales pitch. I don't want to read anyone else's opinion because I don't believe it's real, and they're not me.
>
> It's all about clarity. If it's too fussy or not clear or accurate, I'll just quit. I'm not engaged with it.

How to create better content for autistic people

Make only 1 point in a sentence

Sentences that have only 1 point are easier to understand. This is because the reader doesn't need to think about more than 1 thing at once. Sentences with a lot of information can be overwhelming.

Ask only 1 thing in a question

Sometimes questions refer to more than 1 thing or contain a comparison. For example, I worked on a service that asked people the question 'I prefer a general understanding of a problem to knowing the detail'. This caused problems because some of the autistic research participants found it hard to think about 2 things together and then compare them. If you need to know about multiple things, you can separate the questions, or rephrase so that there is only 1 concept to consider. For example, I rephrased the question above ('I prefer a general understanding of a problem to knowing the detail') to 'I like to focus on details'.

Use facts

Some autistic people prefer to have facts and don't respond well to emotive or persuasive content. For example, sales content could include facts about why the product is worth buying, rather than trying to sell by making a person feel something about a product.

Don't use metaphors and idioms

Some autistic people can interpret things literally, making metaphors, idioms, and jargon confusing. As well as obvious examples like 'over the moon', there are more subtle uses that aren't as easy to detect. For example, I saw an autistic research participant struggle with content that referred to 'feeling stuck' as they immediately thought of being stuck in glue.

There's more about this in 'Figurative language' in chapter 3.

Think carefully about emojis

Emojis can both exclude and be helpful, so you need to think carefully about how to use them. For example, an emoji that is very well known might help to make clear that something is humorous, whereas a lesser-known facial expression might be confusing.

There's more about this in 'Using emojis' in chapter 7.

9
Bipolar disorder and depression

Bipolar disorders are mental health conditions that manifest in mood swings between manic highs and deep, sometimes suicidal, depression. A person with bipolar disorder doesn't always feel very high or very low; they can be anywhere in between. There are also stable periods. Some people describe it as going up and down in waves, and others describe it as a pendulum. Bipolar used to be called manic depression.

The 2014 Adult Psychiatric Morbidity Survey found that bipolar disorders affect about 1 in 50 people in a lifetime.

Psychiatrists categorise bipolar into subtypes. The main subtypes are:

- type 1,
- type 2,
- cyclothymia.

The main differences are that people with type 1 experience full manic episodes, whereas those with type 2 have less intense manic periods called hypomania.

Cyclothymia involves similar symptoms, but these are classed as not severe enough to be diagnosed as type 1 or 2. There are other subtypes, such as rapid cycling bipolar, which is when you cycle through manic episodes and depression more frequently, and bipolar with a seasonal pattern, which means your bipolar is affected by the time of year.

I've included both bipolar and depression in the same chapter because the effects of the bipolar depressive episodes are the same as those of depression.

Depression

Depression is much more common than bipolar and is the most prevalent mental health issue worldwide. The International World Mental Health Survey Initiative estimates that 14% of adults in high-income countries have a major depressive episode in their lifetime.

The intersectionality of mental health is important as systemically excluded groups, unsurprisingly, suffer differently and suffer more.

The Office for National Statistics' 'Disability, wellbeing and loneliness, UK: 2019' report said that disabled people report having lower wellbeing, are more likely to be lonely, and are more likely to have frequent mental distress than people who aren't disabled.

The 2014 Adult Psychiatric Morbidity Survey found that women both report symptoms of and are diagnosed with depression more than men are. A 2021 study found that 1 in 5 mothers experience postpartum depression.

However, according to national statistics for England (2021 to 2022), men are more likely to have substance use disorders and are about 3 times more likely than women to die by suicide. So it could be that men are more likely to self-medicate their depression and less likely to seek help, with devastating consequences. The patriarchy appears to be damaging the mental health of men and women in different and complex ways.

Unfortunately, the statistics just refer to men and women, not other genders. A study by Stonewall found that more than half of LGBTQ+ (lesbian, gay, bisexual, transgender, queer and questioning, and ace) people had experienced depression in the last year. The statistics for transgender people are even higher. Nearly half of transgender people had considered suicide in the last year, which is a devastating statistic.

There is overwhelming evidence that Black women are more likely to experience depression and are less likely to have successful engagement with services because of the discrimination they receive. Black adults have the lowest mental health treatment rate of any ethnic group, despite having a higher prevalence of mental health conditions than the rest of the population.

Black men are more likely to experience psychosis, which can be experienced by people with bipolar disorders. The increased rates of psychosis do not happen in countries with a predominantly Black population, so it is likely a consequence of the environment.

Black British adults are 5 times more likely than white British adults to be detained under the Mental Health Act, which means that they are kept at a facility and may be treated against their wishes. This extreme form of treatment can only be resorted to if someone is assessed as a risk to themselves or others. This chilling statistic has been scrutinised and found to have 'no reason'. Criticism of this finding focuses on the methodology behind it, which did not ask the right questions or include or centre people with lived experience.

How bipolar disorders affect people's lives

Being bipolar can bring times of mania, which is feeling very high and positive. It can also bring depressive episodes, along with times of stability where a person's mood is relatively neutral. It's possible that at times of extreme mania or depression, someone can experience psychosis. Some people experience paranoia.

The effects of bipolar disorders can be managed with medication and therapies. Medication can usually stabilise the mood swings to have more periods of stability and fewer extreme highs and lows.

Mania and hypomania

Mania is a feeling of extremely high energy and elation. It can include psychosis. Hypomania is a less extreme high mood.

When manic or hypomanic, a person can feel on top of the world, confident, and full of creativity and ideas. Some people are massively productive and full of energy.

Everything can move quickly, so a person might have racing thoughts, jump from one thing to another, and get easily distracted by new things. People sometimes either can't or don't want to sleep.

There are some common downsides, like being a bit reckless, spending too much money, or making bad decisions. More extreme manic episodes can involve psychosis, paranoia, and hearing voices.

Depression

Depression always involves low mood, but the depths can vary. It usually means:

- having no energy and feeling tired,
- feeling hopeless,
- not finding things interesting or amusing that someone usually would.

It can be tough to concentrate, get things done, and remember things.

The deeper depths of depression are totally debilitating. There is no positive side to depression.

Sam

Sam has bipolar type 2 and also has epilepsy. He was diagnosed with bipolar in his 20s, but thinks that he probably had it as a teenager or maybe even younger. One of the effects of the bipolar is that he experiences suspicious thoughts and paranoia.

Sam isn't representative of all people with bipolar. These are his own experiences.

> **"**
>
> Bipolar 2 is a mixture of highs and lows.
>
> I take medication, which stems the highs and lows.
>
> My bipolar bleeds itself into other situations. It makes me seem unapologetic and cold and very impatient. I do my best. I can't get that upset, which makes me feel heartless, but I don't have the ability to be that upset. The medication takes the edge off so I struggle to be emotional. I can seem ungrateful because I struggle to feel the highs.
>
> A huge thing with my bipolar is getting very paranoid. I start to believe my own thoughts about people doing or saying things. I can get very worked up about small situations. Things are an irritation, and I lack patience.
>
> People with bipolar have cycles. I have 1 or 2 per year, maybe 3, where I'm either hyper or very depressed with very low thoughts. No medication can stop that. The highs usually last about a week, but the lows are much longer.

I can do so much on a hyper mode, it's ridiculous. I'm like a machine doing things, and I get so much done. But I've also been in situations where I've sat for days and done nothing, and I've lost many days thinking about what I could do and haven't done them. I know when it's coming. I'm good at distracting myself, but I can't usually stop it.

I like things on demand, probably because of my impatience. It's grown over time, so I don't know if it's my fault or technology's fault. Getting what I want there and then suits me.

If I'm on a high, I'll be eager to find more information and get lost in Google and all sorts. On a low, I'll be more dismissive. I'm less interested. How I digest things will be completely different from one day to another. I can think something is useful one day, and the next, I could dismiss it and find everything about it irritating.

What font is used will factor into whether I'll take anything from it. If something is poorly presented or poorly written, I'll dismiss it. The visual representation will be a factor.

If it looks rubbish like old internet Times New Roman I'll be dismissive. I'm not willing to understand the content because it looks unappealing.

A highly polished website that looks good and has polished writing is more appealing. Visuals are important.

It's off-putting when something is very plain because there's an air of suspicion. What aren't they saying? It's so plain and basic and to the point. When I'm on a lower ebb, a bit of paranoia comes in, and it makes me feel uneasy, thinking, 'what are they really saying?'

If I am feeling fine, I'd have no problem with it. I could absorb it for what it is.

When I'm at a higher ebb, I wouldn't care, but there's the suspicion when I'm lower, and I spend more of my time on the lower ebb. This is too basic. What am I missing? Where is it? Is it hidden within it? It's so basic I'm looking for something more complicated. It's fine most of the time, but not when I'm feeling low.

For example, government websites with basic information are distracting. I find it a bit Oxbridge public school. This is the basic information, and you will read it, and that's all you need to know.

I find timers horrendous, really distracting—the pressure to get it done. If I'm buying tickets, it gives you 5 minutes. I feel pressurised, and I hate it. Recalling information can be not ideal, and I can get wound up about it. There's a pressure of that constraint, and I don't like it. It's like being on the Crystal Maze, and I need to get it done in time. I think, 'I haven't got time for this' when I have got time, I've got all the time in the world, but it makes me irritable and affects my demeanour.

If I was feeling higher, I'd be chilled out about it, but a website timer would be irritant if I were at a lower ebb. If I was very low, I wouldn't go through it, and I wouldn't buy the tickets.

If things seem complicated, I'll put it off until the last possible moment. I'll put it off and put it off. Sometimes, if there is a deadline, I'll just have forgotten by then. If I'm feeling better, I'll just do it. But even then, when things are impending, it can make me irritable.

I'll ignore things until it goes away or until I'm reminded. When I was remortgaging, I put it off until I forgot about it. It lapsed, and they doubled the payment. It cost me financially because I put it off so much.

The form was an atrocious, horrible drop-down form. There was certain language in the form where I'd think, 'what does that word actually mean?' Because of how I am, I'd think, 'do they mean that? Are they trying to trick me?' A bit of paranoia creeps in. It was so off-putting. My paranoia about banks made me wonder if they're doing it on purpose.

It is common that people with bipolar disorder would rather have it than not. I see the world as black and white, and I find it difficult to see grey areas. I can see through a situation and get to the end, and that's fantastic. It gives me a certain bit of vision. My concentration can be in the right area, not in grey areas, so I don't get distracted. I can see through ambiguities. Not seeing the grey can be upsetting for others. It's the truth and nothing else, offensive or not.

> My black and whiteness makes me distrust ambiguous things. What is the hidden agenda? I won't want to read it if I'm on a lower ebb. If it's not black and white, it causes mistrust. When there's a lot of long words that aren't needed and flowery over-explaining with too much description, I'll distrust it and think there's something hidden. Sometimes I can read a whole paragraph and think I still don't know anything, so it needs to be more to the point. I need a certain level of pedanticness, but if it's a bit much, I distrust it, and it will put me off. But if it's too basic, I think, 'is that it? I know that', and I'll distrust it. I need a middle ground.

How to create better content for people with bipolar disorders and depression

Many ways to help create inclusive content for people with bipolar and depression are covered by the neurodiversity recommendations in chapter 8. These points are particularly useful:

- give reminders and let people know where they are in a service,
- don't expect people to remember things,
- put all the essential information upfront.

Some additional points are particularly important for those with bipolar disorders and depression.

Avoid using timers

Making someone complete a task within a set time can be stressful. Even if the time available is generous, it can make them feel uneasy. When someone is depressed, it can feel impossible to do things that might seem simple at other times, and a timer is another barrier that can cause them to give up.

Avoid ambiguity

Ambiguous content is hard work. It's unlikely that anyone intentionally creates vague content, but there are common issues that lead to ambiguity, such as:

- complicated words,
- jargon,
- meandering sentences,
- writing in the passive voice.

These things can make content ambiguous because they stop content from being clear. Ambiguity can lead to mistrust. For people who experience suspicious thoughts or paranoia, ambiguity can be distressing.

10
Aphasia

Aphasia is a language impairment caused by an injury to the left side of the brain. This is the side of the brain that controls communication.

About a third of people who survive a stroke have aphasia. It can be caused by any type of brain trauma like a tumour, dementia, or head injury.

Aphasia makes it hard to use language. It can affect:

- reading,
- writing,
- speaking,
- understanding,
- non-verbal communication.

Aphasia affects people differently, and the severity and combinations of difficulties vary from person to person.

It doesn't affect intelligence or the way someone thinks.

The Stroke Association estimates that about 350,000 people in the UK live with aphasia. The National Aphasia Association estimates that about 2 million people in the United States are living with aphasia.

The condition can make someone feel lonely and frustrated, and it takes its toll on their mental health.

Speech and language therapy helps to regain the language skills that have been affected by brain trauma.

How aphasia affects people's lives

Because communication is so central, aphasia can profoundly affect someone's life.

At the more 'mild' end of the spectrum, someone may speak well but have difficulties reading or writing. Someone at the more severe end, with what is known as 'global aphasia', may not be able to speak, read, write, or understand what they hear. Some may learn to communicate through gestures, and others may find even gestures difficult.

Aphasia does not affect intelligence, but because it is due to a brain injury, some people have cognitive difficulties because a different part of their brain was damaged. The injury may also have affected parts of the brain that affect physical movement.

It's common for people who have had strokes to have weakness on the right side of their body and visual impairment of the right eye. This is because the left side of the brain controls the right side of the body.

Because aphasia affects people in such different ways, I have included 2 personal stories. Both Colin and Howard have relatively mild aphasia, and Howard also has apraxia. People with severe aphasia are unlikely to use standard websites and apps, even with accessibility tools.

Colin and Howard aren't representative of all people with aphasia. These are their own experiences.

Colin

Colin is the founder of the charity Say Aphasia. He runs it with the support of friends who also have aphasia.

He had a stroke in 2013, which resulted in him becoming aphasic.

Colin was 50 when he had his stroke, and he could no longer continue in his successful career, at a huge cost to him and his family.

He founded Say Aphasia to continue a much-needed support group after another charity closed down.

Say Aphasia is a huge success and now has support groups across Sussex and in the North East, Wales, and Yorkshire. There are also virtual groups.

Colin is an extremely positive and determined person and runs the charity to help others like him.

> ❝
>
> I had a stroke about 8 years ago, and in the hospital, I could only say yes, no, and swear words.
>
> I had to relearn all of my words. I had to learn to talk again.
>
> My intelligence was intact, and most people are the same. I would like to say something, but I couldn't get it out. The words are there, but it's like an electrical thing stopping them. I'd know exactly what phrase I wanted to say, but I just couldn't get the right words

out. I might know I want to say 'I'm alright', but I couldn't get the words 'I'm alright' out, so I would do a thumbs up.

I can have conversations now. Some of the words aren't quite right. One of the things I can't do is 'he's', 'she's', 'him', and 'hers'. They're just words. I've tried different ways, but it's just not happening.

When I was having speech and language therapy, it took about a year to understand my aphasia and what was going on with my brain. Now I can talk again and have conversations, but I can't read and can't write.

Through my charity, we run support groups. We've got at least 150 to 200 people coming to groups, and they are all different. Some people can't say a whole sentence. A lot of people can read but can't write. Some people can write but can't read. Some are half paralysed, and as it's a right-side weakness, they have to be left-handed, which isn't easy.

People have brain injuries other than strokes. Some have tumours. One person who runs a group had a car crash. Everyone is so different.

I have voice recognition on my iPhone. That's how I set up my charity. If I haven't got the exact words, I know it's not quite right. I can't see where it's wrong, so I have to delete it all and start again. It takes a long time to do emails and texts.

I practised my words with my sister and practised sending texts. It was good for me to practise so that I could do a text with a whole sentence. The first email I did took about 6 hours. Now it's much easier.

There are many apps for people with aphasia to practise their words or do it for us.

If I have an email, the voice recognition tells me what's going on. For example, I'll say, 'Hi, how are you?', and it does it for me. If I've got a text, I can read some of the words, but it gets confusing, so the voice recognition does it for me.

Everything that I do is on my phone. I have lots of apps. Doing anything the old-fashioned way doesn't work for me. I can't do it.

If I look at some news sites on my phone, if there's anything that I don't understand, I can use the phone to read it for me. But other news sites don't work that way. I do get very annoyed. I want to talk to the people who make these sites and say, 'a lot of people have brain injuries, and they can't read it!'. Everyone should be able to access all of these things, and if it's not working on the speak thing, I get very frustrated.

The worst thing that I have to use is the website for the government. It is crap. Why can't they make it easier? It's so complicated that my brain is just going to explode.

I had to get a new driving licence, and I tried to do it online. I couldn't do it. If you look at the website, it says that it's easy to see what's going on. So I look at my iPhone, and it's so complicated. I get very confused. It is absolutely terrible.

I would like to get the email address for the government and say, 'there are 350 thousand people with aphasia. Please just make sure online access is accessible'. But it's just not going to happen.

There are lots of websites for people with aphasia. Some are pretty good because there are the words, but they have pictures and videos as well. It makes it much easier, but there aren't any on other websites or apps.

Language needs to be easy for everyone with aphasia. It needs to be simple and easy. If it's too complicated, then you can just forget about it. We can't do it.

Headlines are good for us. When I'm reading a sentence, by the time I have got to the last word, it has taken a long time, but I still don't know what it is. Research shows that headlines and pictures are much easier to understand for people with aphasia. When you have pictures, if the words are getting a bit too complicated, then you have something else to work out what they're saying.

"

Howard

Howard has both aphasia and apraxia. Apraxia of speech affects the brain pathways that plan the physical movement of speech. Like aphasia, someone knows what they want to say, but can't properly plan and sequence the movements.

Howard is a retired IT director and did a degree in astronomy and astrophysics when he was 60.

He had a stroke 2 and a half years ago and credits his hugely supportive wife and family for helping him recover from his stroke and relearn how to communicate.

Howard attends his local Say Aphasia support group and finds fun ways to fundraise for the charity.

> **"**
>
> I had a stroke in October 2019. I had to learn to speak again and read and write again, which was really hard. I have a supportive family that has helped me. My memory is good, and my ability is good; my only problems are language and speaking.
>
> Immediately after the stroke, I didn't have any words, nothing, and it was really frustrating. For 2 days after the stroke, I had nothing. Then, on the third day, my words came back in my head, but I couldn't speak.
>
> For 4 days, I didn't know anything about the right-hand side of my body. I didn't know what my right hand was. For 1 or 2 weeks, my right hand was clawed up, and I had weakness in my right leg, but that recovered quickly.

I could understand but not communicate. I tried to communicate through drawing with limited success. I'm right-handed. I think I'm naturally left-handed, but my mother trained me to use my right hand, so I managed okay with my left hand. I use my right hand again now.

I find the words 'apraxia' and 'aphasia' difficult. The long words. Words that don't sound like how they are spelt.

Apraxia is a motor condition; it's the movements for speech. It means not knowing how to form the word to get it out physically. So I have problems with 2 things: one to say it and one to physically form the word, so 2 processes are difficult.

My writing is now good, but it took time. 2 weeks after the stroke, I could write in a simplistic way. It came back relatively quickly. Learning to read again was really hard and took longer. I now read complex books, but it takes much longer than it used to.

I had NHS speech therapy for 6 to 8 months.

My reading is slow. I have to reread things.

I use a phone, an iPad, a laptop – everything. I find using them really good. I use them differently now than I used to because I have to concentrate more now.

I sometimes use voice recognition. I used it a lot more in the beginning, but less now. To read, I have to make it speak sometimes.

I do everything on a device. Shopping, reading the news, WhatsApp, Facebook, Facetime and Zoom. Everything.

Sometimes when I'm looking at the news, the headlines are confusing. I have to go down to see what happened. Things that don't have the correct punctuation are confusing.

I have problems with using search. I can't find the right words for what I want to find, so using Google is really hard.

I found taxing the car easy. I'm doing a tax return now, and I can't do it. There are too many questions and answers. It's too hard.

Sometimes I have to really concentrate and break up sentences. I sometimes have to look at every word and put it together. It depends if the words are complicated. I need to keep it simple.

Sometimes I have issues with reading aloud (a screen reader) because it's too slow, and I have problems with an accent. The odd nuances catch me when it's reading to me in a different adaptation, like American.

I have to do things slowly. My mind is fast, but now things are slow. It's frustrating.

Please don't use double negatives. I can't do them.

Photos are good for me; pictures and illustrations help, as do videos, but videos take longer.

Aphasia

> I need sentences broken down with the right punctuation, so there aren't long sentences. I need 1 option in each sentence. It's important only to have 1 at a time.

Aphasia and mental health

Living with aphasia is a frustrating and often lonely experience.

Research has shown that 70% of people who have had aphasia for 3 months have depression. After 12 months with aphasia, 62% of people have depression, which is a small drop from 70%. Despite the drop, the proportion of those whose depression is severe increased over that time.

I spoke to Dr Anna Caute of Essex University, who lectures on Speech and Language Therapy. Her main research interest is the use of technology in aphasia therapy.

Anna has many fascinating insights that I use throughout this chapter.

Anna gave me some insight into mental health.

> **"**
>
> Having aphasia is a risk factor for depression. It makes sense because it affects your life and your ability to talk about what's going on. It affects people's ability to access psychological therapy, because if you're offered talking therapy, you won't necessarily be able to access it. Anxiety is also common.
>
> Research has also looked at the impact of aphasia on social relationships, which is closely related. Communication impairments affect people's ability to make contact. One study looked at people with chronic aphasia, and on average, they have 3 friends, but 3% of people saw no friends, and most people see their friends less than before the diagnosis.
>
> **"**

How to create better content for people living with aphasia

Following the recommendations in 'Structure and styling' in chapter 4 and 'Clear language' in chapter 3 will help people with aphasia.

There has been some fantastic research on improving digital experiences for those with aphasia.

The Stroke Association funded a research project run by the University of Sheffield. The project resulted in the Stroke Association Accessible Information Guidelines.

The guidelines are a practical guide on how to create accessible content and were co-designed with people with aphasia. They are excellent, and I highly recommend that you read them.

The guidelines echo the general good practice of plain language and readability, but they go further on some aspects. For example, they recommend that simple sentences should be about 5 words, rather than the usual recommended 15 to 20.

Let people choose how they receive information

Because people with aphasia can have any combination of problems with speaking, understanding what they hear, reading, and writing, they need options for how they receive digital content. For example, it might be better for them to read it, listen to it, or see it explained by pictures or in a video.

It's important to give people options, so they can use as many or as few channels as they need.

Considerate Content

Dr Anna Caute speaks about the importance of having choices when reading or listening to content.

> **"**
>
> Someone could have good auditory comprehension, but their reading comprehension could be affected.
>
> I've researched e-readers, screen readers, and software such as text-to-speech, which reads aloud. These tools can have a massive impact on people's lives. It can mean the difference between being able to read a book or not, or being able to read the news.
>
> But a lot of people have both auditory and reading comprehension difficulties. We've seen in practice that a lot of those people benefit from dual input. So even if they have impaired understanding of spoken language and impaired reading, having both channels together is helpful.
>
> For example, on a Kindle, people can download an audiobook and then link it to the written version, so they can listen to someone reading and follow the text at the same time. People find that helpful because it's a human voice rather than a mechanical, digital voice. The combination of following the text and listening can help people even if they have an impaired understanding of language.
>
> It won't help everybody. Having 2 information channels is cognitively harder for some people, who may find that distracting. But for a lot of people, having those 2 channels helps them.
>
> **"**

Use pictures and videos

People with aphasia need information to be conveyed in the simplest way possible. For some, reading will be fine, or listening will be fine, but for others, these options will be too complicated, and pictures or videos would be more accessible.

The Stroke Association Information Accessibility Guidelines give details on using pictures to convey information.

Their guidelines on how to link writing and pictures are:

- put the picture under the sentence,
- check the picture matches the important information exactly,
- use a new picture for new information,
- use 2 pictures if you need to,
- use a new picture for each new concept.

Their recommendations for a good picture is one where the:

- people look right (adult and old enough),
- picture shows the activity,
- picture matches the words.

Let people hear content in a human voice

It's easy to assume that people who need to hear content instead of reading it can use a screen reader to read it aloud. However, Dr Anna Caute spoke about the importance of having the option of hearing a human voice rather than having to rely on a screen reader.

There are 2 issues with screen readers:

- the digital or mechanical voice is difficult for some people,
- screen readers can be hard to use, particularly if you have problems with dexterity.

> **"**
>
> With e-readers like Kindle, you can listen to a book with text-to-speech, but that sounds like a digital voice, whereas with an audiobook, you're listening to a real human reading it aloud. People much prefer the real human voice. Could that happen on websites, too? Could they have someone read aloud each page? That would make it much easier to listen to and much more accessible.
>
> Some things may sound unnatural on a screen reader with a digital voice. If it's something specific, like a government website, I don't see why you couldn't get someone to read each section aloud. You could click on it and listen, and it would also be helpful to highlight the text so that people can follow.
>
> If you're reading on an iPad, it will speak the text for you, but you have to click, hold, select, and then press speak, which is quite challenging in terms of dexterity. It would be helpful to have a clear icon and a text label that said 'Read aloud' on a web page. You click on it, and then it reads that chunk for you.
>
> **"**

11

Deafblindness

Deafblindness is a combination of hearing loss and sight loss.

It doesn't mean that someone can't hear or see at all. Most deafblind people have some hearing, sight, or both.

According to figures by Sense, a UK charity, about 450,000 people in the UK are deafblind. This figure is expected to rise to 610,000 by 2035. Ageing is the most common cause of deafblindness.

Deafblindness has many causes other than ageing. Some examples are:

- Usher syndrome,
- CHARGE syndrome,
- congenital rubella syndrome,
- medical complications during pregnancy and birth, including cerebral palsy,
- an illness or accident.

How deafblindness affects people's lives

The combination of the 2 sensory impairments affects people in many different ways.

In the UK, the Department of Health has described deafblindness as sight and hearing loss that often causes 'difficulties with communication, access to information, and mobility'.

Communication and access to information will vary significantly from person to person, and deafblind people may use a combination of speech, touch, sign, or visual languages that work best in any particular situation.

Aids for sight loss

Various aids can help someone with sight loss to access digital content, such as:

- screen magnification,
- screen readers,
- braille display.

Screen magnifiers

Magnifying the screen can be useful for people who have some sight. Screen magnifiers enlarge the size of what someone sees on the screen. Depending on the screen magnifier, they will either zoom in on sections or enlarge the whole screen.

Most devices and computers have screen magnifiers built-in as an accessibility feature. This is not the same as zooming in through your browser, which you can do with hand gestures on a phone, tablet, or trackpad.

There are apps and software with more features you can buy, such as ZoomText and Supernova, but some are pretty expensive. The software you pay for usually has additional features like changing the cursor and colours so that you can customise it to suit your needs.

Screen readers

Screen readers convert the text into either a synthetic voice (this means computer-generated) or braille. They allow someone to navigate and read the text, and use keyboard shortcuts to run through headings and links.

Most devices and computers have a screen reader built-in as an accessibility feature; for example, Apple VoiceOver, Microsoft Narrator, and TalkBack for Android.

You can also buy screen-reading software with more features, such as JAWS (Job Access with Speech).

Screen readers can help deafblind people who have some hearing, as well as those who read braille and use a braille display.

Braille display

The population of people who use braille is relatively small. Still, braille is an absolute lifeline in communication for some people, so it's crucial to consider people using braille when creating content. Another tactile form of printing is Moon.

Refreshable braille or 'paperless braille' lets someone read digital content through touch. Screen readers translate the content to braille using electronic refreshable braille displays, creating the braille dots by pins moving up and down. Refreshable braille hardware is expensive, generally ranging between £1,000 and £5,000.

Text-to-speech

Text-to-speech and screen readers aren't the same. Text-to-speech reads aloud digital content but doesn't usually let you collate headings and hyperlinks into lists. You usually operate text-to-speech with a mouse or your hand if using a device, and you can't use the keyboard shortcuts that you would use with a screen reader.

Hearing aids and implants

Some deafblind people use a hearing aid or implant.

People can use hearing aids if they have some hearing. They don't give a person perfect hearing but can make significant improvements by making sounds louder and clearer.

People can use implants when hearing aids wouldn't work, usually for more profound and permanent hearing loss. They work in different ways depending on the reason for the hearing loss.

Molly

Molly is 27 years old and has Usher syndrome. She is a usability and accessibility consultant, specialising in assistive technology and design for those with sensory impairments.

Molly is passionate about technology and creating a positive impact.

Molly isn't representative of all deafblind people. These are her own experiences.

> ❝
>
> I am deafblind due to a condition called Usher syndrome. Usher syndrome is the most common cause of congenital deafblindness. You're born deaf, and you acquire blindness, usually through adolescence. There are a few different types and subtypes. Mine is type 2, where you have a severe hearing loss, and then through adolescence, the blindness kicks in. The blindness of Usher syndrome is called retinitis pigmentosa, also known as RP.
>
> You experience a deterioration in your peripheral vision. It's often called tunnel vision, but it's not really. The rate of progression depends on the person. Some people can get to a point where their vision stays stable, but others aren't as lucky.
>
> I went from being partially sighted at the age of 12 to severely sight impaired, which is another way of saying blind, at the age of 14. I have around 5 degrees of vision left, which I rely on.

I'm still very visual. I use lots of large text and zoom. I use screen readers, but I'm not relying on them yet. I use all sorts of technology to help me in my day-to-day life.

I was given my first pair of hearing aids at 18 months old. I went from analogue to digital hearing aids at 8 or 9. That was the first time I heard birds singing and leaves crunching. When I was 20, I was introduced to smart hearing aid technology. The clarity of sounds is so much better. I have an app with Bluetooth connectivity to stream calls and music, which I couldn't do before.

My hearing aids have improved my speech. As the hearing aid technology has gotten better, my voice and communication skills have also improved.

I wear my hearing aids every single day, and I couldn't be without them. They stream through to my iPhone and my Apple watch, and I use them for navigation. If I'm going to meet a client at a coffee shop, for example, I put it into Maps. The map talks to me through my hearing aid and also vibrates. It tells me to turn left or right. It's not necessarily assistive tech, but it's an amazing technology that's implemented accessibility well.

I use the whole Apple ecosystem. The accessibility features are so consistent. They all talk to each other, which is great. For reading, I prefer using the Kindle rather than an iPad. I don't like the backlight on the iPad. I like the Kindle without the backlight. I use the one that looks like a page of a book, and you can adjust the font size and contrast. That's enough for me.

I use lots of technologies that link with my iPhone. My hearing aids also connect to a TV streamer. I don't want to sit too close as that will hurt my eyes, so I'll stream the TV to my ears, which is cool. I also have a mini multi-mic that is Bluetooth connected to my iPhone and my hearing aids. So if I'm in a meeting, and we've got bad acoustics, or it's very busy, I can put it on the table and set it to hear everyone around the table. That's a really handy piece of kit that I take with me when I go away.

I use my Apple for everything vision-related, like zoom magnification and colour filters. I change the colours, and dim the screen brightness and contrast.

There are a couple of screen readers on iPhone devices. There's one called VoiceOver, and there's one called Speak Screen. I'm more likely to use Speak Screen, which no one ever talks about. I can swipe 2 fingers down, and it will read the content. I can pause it and speed it up. That's a very useful speaking tool.

I'll use a screen reader when I'm tired, or struggling to access an app. Online shopping, for instance, is inaccessible. I installed an app the other day, and I could not follow or read anything. Even zooming in and the contrast was terrible. I turned on VoiceOver to gauge what was going on, but the app hadn't been built to work with that either. It said 'button, button, button', so things weren't labelled properly.

Some things aren't built to work with a screen reader. For example, if it's big blocks of text, I would use a screen reader to relax my eyes. Also, sometimes, if it's bright or dark. I have good days and bad days with my sight, so on the bad days, I'm more likely to use screen readers.

A lot of the problems are with contrast colour and text spacing. I will try to adjust the colour filters feature on my iPhone, but it is really hard to override the colour palettes on some websites. You can invert colours to a darker background, avoiding it being black with white. But if you have a blue website with pink writing, and then you invert it, you can get some strange, like, neon stuff going on, which is not helpful at all. I often find that if the colours and contrast are okay, I can enlarge or zoom in even if the text is too small. That's more of a comfortable experience, rather than having these awful contrasting colours.

I often make the text larger in the browser, and sometimes when you do that, the text falls off the screen.

A lot of the problems with screen readers is navigational. The toolbar and the drop-down menus can be hard to use on a keyboard.

I find it difficult when there are massive titles, and then the subtext is tiny, so there's a massive difference in size. I get that you need a title larger than the rest, but I don't like it when it's a drastic difference. I don't like that. Also, when fonts are too close together or too far apart, it all flows together. They merge into a blur. That's why contrast is really important.

> Videos that aren't captioned and are automatically played can be a real challenge—and annoying for everyone.
>
> Another thing is transcripts. If you have a video on a website, some caption it but don't offer a transcript. Some people who are deafblind need a transcript. If you're captioning your videos, why not have a transcript as well? Both do a good job.
>
> Podcasts are now a big thing. If you're doing a podcast, you could be speaking into something that is writing what you're saying, and you can correct it later. There are so many podcasts where the topics are hugely interesting for all the communities out there. It's offensive to just not automatically include these people. Make sure the content is accessible. It's not that hard.
>
> 🗩

How to create better content for deafblind people

People who are deafblind can have any level of sight loss and hearing loss. The most important thing is not to assume how a person will want to consume content and to give options. For example, someone might be okay using a screen magnifier in good light and when they feel well, but want to use text-to-speech instead if their eyes are tired or there's a lot to read.

Links and buttons

When someone is using a screen reader, they don't always have it read every word out loud. In the same way that someone with sight might skip and scan a page, a screen reader user may skip through the content, focusing on links, headings and buttons.

Make sure that links and buttons are fully descriptive so they stand independently. For example, a link that says 'read the full returns policy' is more helpful than 'for returns click here', which tells a person nothing if they're skipping through the links with a screen reader.

Headings

Label headings correctly so that the hierarchy of the page is clear to someone using a screen reader, as well as someone who can see.

Headings should be labelled from H1 through to H6 without skipping any levels in the hierarchy. For example, don't skip a heading style and go from H1 to H3 because H2 looks too big.

You should follow the headings hierarchy without thinking

about their appearance. Use headings instead of using bold or increasing the font size.

Content for people who use braille

One of the simplest and most effective ways to ensure that text is translated well into braille is to ensure that the structure of the page is implemented correctly so that the hierarchy is apparent without seeing it. For example, make sure that headings and links are labelled as such and are descriptive.

There's more information on how to do this in chapter 4.

Braille can't translate images, so make sure to use good alt-text and describe the insights in graphs or tables.

Write alternative text (alt-text) for images

Screen readers can't translate images, so we must include text alternatives to any images we use. Read more about how to write good alt-text in 'How to write good alt-text' in chapter 5.

Don't use text over images

It's hard to read words over the top of images because of the varying contrast. Read more about why images that contain text are problematic in 'Images that contain text' in chapter 5.

Use transcripts and captions

All audio (for example, podcasts) needs a transcript so that those who can't hear can read the content instead.

Videos should have captions so people can read instead of listen.

You can read more about using transcripts and captions in chapter 6.

Consider sign language

Consider including a sign language video to interpret the content. Remember that sign language is its own language and culture. If you're not familiar with it, speak to a charity or organisation that works with sign language users. There may be specific things you need to consider. It's not usually as straightforward as just translating a page of English content into sign language.

You can find out more in 'Sign language' in Chapter 6.

Workshop

Naming things

Naming things is hard.

There are many reasons why it is so hard to name things, but top of the list is that people can feel emotional about names in a way they would not about other aspects of their work.

Who has the responsibility for naming something is often an issue. For example, a founder might feel strongly about the name of their brand when it is objectively a bad name.

Other reasons why it can be hard to name something are:

- the thing that needs a name does not have a clear purpose,
- some people like names to be funny, cool, or clever,
- some people want the name to make a good acronym.

Content people are sometimes called on to help with naming things because they are seen as 'word people' who can think of something creative or funny. However, we should advocate that names be descriptive and help the people to understand what the thing is.

Considerate naming is vital for both comprehension and inclusion.

How to make a Jamaican laugh

I thought I'd include a daft story as an example. My partner is Jamaican, and once, for a reason I don't remember, I mentioned the company Babylon Health. If you've never heard of them, they are a UK-based private digital healthcare company.

The words 'BABYLON. HEALTH?!' were barely audible through the laughter. 'That's a joke, right?'

If you don't know, Babylon is what Rastafari people call 'the system', capitalism, the police, white colonialism, the oppressor. You get the picture. To my partner, Babylon Health was basically called Evil Capitalist Health. The UK has a National Health Service, which is mostly free, and people are highly suspicious of private healthcare companies, so it's a bit awkward.

Sorry, Babylon Health.

Naming services that the public need to use

Services that need to be used by the public should have descriptive names that are also verbs. This makes the service name the same as the task the person wants to do.

This makes the service findable.

In the UK, there is a government service standard with really clear guidelines on naming your service.

The guidelines outline that good service names:

- use the words the people using that service use,
- are based on analytics and user research,
- describe a task, not a technology,
- don't need to change when policy or technology changes,
- are verbs, not nouns,
- don't include government department or agency names,
- aren't brand-driven or focused on marketing.

These guidelines are evidenced and used across the UK government and are a great place to start with naming any publicly used service.

People won't find the service without a clear, descriptive name.

Naming internal services

Problems sometimes arise when naming internal services, as they are usually given to people to use. It's less common that people have to find them.

I've witnessed various representations made as to why a particular internal service should stray from the guidelines. Examples are that people are used to a name (or an acronym) or that a verb doesn't make sense for a staff system. It's true that the staff don't have to find the service from Google, but they still need to know what it is and what it does. A descriptive name is the easiest way to do that.

As you can't rely on Google analytics to tell you what the name should be from search terms, it's important to do user research with your staff. The important thing is that they understand what it is and what it does, not whether they like the name.

If it's hard to name something using the UK government guidelines, that might mean that the thing isn't a service, it lacks purpose, or that it's meeting a bunch of different needs in one place. Or worst case scenario: it's not meeting any needs.

If you are committed to user-centred design, these guidelines should apply to both internal and external services. Staff systems should be designed around staff needs, which should make it relatively simple to name them.

Naming things using acronyms and abbreviations

Acronyms and abbreviations are an easy but unhelpful way to name things.

It's hard work to give something a proper descriptive name as you have to work out precisely what it does and why. You have to carefully consider what problem it's solving.

It can be easier to use an acronym that stands for 2, 3, or 4 nondescript words. This is common, particularly for internal systems. Unfortunately, this easy naming strategy usually ends with the people having no idea what it is or where to find it.

Always argue for a descriptive name.

Team names

Team names might seem a bit of an aside in the context of this book, but content people are often involved with helping their teams communicate clearly, and team names are about communication.

Naming teams is a bit of a canary-in-the-coal-mine situation. They can easily reveal a culture that is not driven by inclusion.

As a general rule, team names should be the same as the function, product, or service name. This means all your colleagues know what the team is doing, and they don't have to remember random team names. It makes things simple.

The main exception is when a project is in a discovery phase, and the product or service hasn't been defined yet. The team shouldn't have a name that leads to or leans towards a solution in discovery. If you've come up with a mission statement and a problem statement, that might help you to come up with a team name that's not solution-based.

A random team name can be helpful if you can't come up with a name that isn't tainted by anticipated solutions.

Random team names must be inclusive.

If there's an in-joke or a reference that you may or may not get, it's not inclusive.

As an example, Star Wars characters, football teams, and soap stars aren't inclusive. Neither are vintage cars, football players, obscure bands from the '80s, Pokémon, or basically anything fun. It might be fun for you, but it's almost certainly not fun for everyone. A team name shouldn't be anything you have to 'get'. Someone might not want to be a stormtrooper as much as you don't want to be Lisa from Dirty Dancing.

Things like colours, oceans, and continents are inclusive. It might not seem as fun, but neither is feeling like a misfit because you have no idea who some random TV character is. Nobody likes a clique.

As soon as you know what the product or service is, the team should take on that name.

Big services with multiple feature teams

Sometimes a service is too big for one multidisciplinary team and has to be divided up. There's no reason why the team names and service names shouldn't still be descriptive.

The big service itself should be pretty easy to name. I'm assuming that the service is understood quite well if it has been deemed too big for one team.

The 'feature teams' might be more tricky. Sometimes people want the team to stay the same and have the same name when they move on to build a new feature.

The simplest thing to do is for the team to be named descriptively after the thing they're doing. As an example, 'Book an appointment for a visa interview' could be a feature team of an entire 'Apply to come to the United Kingdom' service (I have no idea if this is a real service; sorry, Home Office). Then, if the team move on to build something else, the team name can change to reflect that.

Run a naming workshop

If you have problems agreeing on a name for a product or service, you could run a naming workshop to reach an agreement.

I saw a talk by Tom Hewitson on 'name storms' at a conference and have been using this rough structure since. It's always worked well.

Book the right people in

You need to schedule it for 90 minutes to make sure you don't run out of time. It's essential to make a decision at the end of the workshop, so don't skimp on time. It will be a false economy.

If you are working in a multidisciplinary team, invite the whole team, not just the people who have a strong opinion.

If you can invite anyone who might use the product or service, that would be brilliant.

Invite stakeholders who will have an opinion on the name. If anyone can veto a decision, they must be in the room for the workshop. You don't want to waste everyone's time reaching a decision only for it to be overruled.

You need a big enough space that has a whiteboard or space on the walls for flip-chart paper. A flip-chart won't be big enough.

If you're working remotely, you can use a digital tool that works for all the participants.

The workshop itinerary

Start by introducing what will happen and ask everyone to agree that you will make a final decision at the end of the workshop.

You will need sticky notes and pens for everyone.

Part 1: Run through who is expected to use the product or service and their needs

If you have a user researcher on the team, they are a good person to run through who will use it and their needs in relation to the product or service. You only need a quick overview to remind people. Everyone should know this stuff already.

Part 2: Decide on the rules

You need a set of rules that the name will comply with. You will use these later on in the workshop to narrow down your options.

As an example, the rules could be that the name needs to:

- be self-explanatory,
- be descriptive,
- start with a verb (for services, maybe not for some products),
- use common words, not jargon.

Everyone needs to be on board with the rules. Otherwise, you might not be able to get a final decision on the name.

Part 3: Ideas

Have 5 minutes for everyone to write down all their ideas for the name, one idea per sticky note.

If people are still going after 5 minutes, carry on until all the inspiration has dried up.

Get everyone to put all their sticky notes up on the whiteboard or wall.

Part 4: Eliminate the names that aren't appropriate
Revisit the rules and eliminate everything that doesn't comply.

Take the sticky notes that don't meet the rules off the board and put them to one side.

Get everyone involved in this. If anyone has put something on that doesn't comply with the rules and wants to rewrite it, let them do that. There will likely be some good ideas that just need a tweak.

Part 5: Vote
Dot voting works well for this. Give everyone 3 votes and get them to put a dot on the 3 they like the most. Everyone can distribute the dots however they like and can put them all on the same sticky note if they love it.

If you have a person or people in the room who everyone feels should have more weight in the decision, maybe give them more votes.

Throw away all the sticky notes with no votes.

Part 6: Advocate
Ask everyone to advocate for their favourite.

If nobody feels strongly enough to fight for it, then set it aside.

At this point, you likely will only have a few options.

Part 7: Context

Take the remaining options and throw them around in some sentences and see how they work. Then as a group, make a decision.

Keep the remaining options as back-up.

Done. Happy days.

Conclusion

Considerate Content

In Part 1 we started by discussing the research I've been part of and how it defined my content work. The guidance in Part 2 should help you work out how to improve your content in ways that work for the fantastic people who shared their experiences with you in Part 3, and most other people as well.

I hope that you feel motivated and enlightened by the case studies in Part 3 and that they help inform your future content decisions. Maybe the personal experiences could trigger some questions for you.

How would this long explanation work for Paul? Would he get this far? Is there something else on the page that could distract him?

How would Jane cope with this long sentence when she has to read it 3 times?

Would Naomi understand this emoji?

How would this timer affect Sam? Would it put him off making the purchase?

How would Howard get to the information he needs through this search function? Could we give him an alternative route so that he can find it?

How could Molly understand what is happening in this video on a day when she wants to use a screen reader?

And many more.

Some points about improving content may seem small, even trivial, to some people. I'd argue that is absolutely not the case. You have the power to make people's lives a little easier and help them feel more welcome with what you produce. And what a wonderful gift that is.

Further reading, references, and attributions

Introduction
- Web Content Accessibility Guidelines (WCAG). https://www.w3.org

Chapter 1
- World Health Organization (2022). 'Global report on health equity for persons with disabilities'.
- 'The Department of Work and Pensions Family Resources Survey (2021/22). https://www.gov.uk/government/statistics/family-resources-survey-financial-year-2021-to-2022
- 2021 American Community Survey – 1 year estimates https://data.census.gov/table/ACSST1Y2021.S1810?q=s1810
- Centres for Disease Control and Prevention. https://www.cdc.gov/ncbddd/disabilityandhealth/data.html

Chapter 3
- Jarrett, Caroline. 'Why plain language and Plain English are different'. https://www.effortmark.co.uk/why-plain-language-and-plain-english-are-different/
- International Plain Language Federation. https://www.iplfederation.org/plain-language/

Chapter 4
- Nielson, Jakob (1997). 'How Users Read on the Web'. https://www.nngroup.com/articles/how-users-read-on-the-web/
- The Readability Guidelines. https://readabilityguidelines.co.uk/

Chapter 6
- The Readability Guidelines. https://readabilityguidelines.co.uk/
- Portlock, Zoe. 'A guide to using subtitles, captions and transcripts for accessibility'. https://business.scope.org.uk/article/subtitles-closed-captions-transcripts-and-accessibility
- Ofcom Podcast Survey (2023). https://www.ofcom.org.uk/about-ofcom/our-research/stats23

Chapter 7
- Full Emoji List. unicode.org
- Coats, Steven (2018). 'Skin Tone Emoji and Sentiment on Twitter'.
- Robertson, Alexander; Magdy, Walid; and Goldwater, Sharon (2021). 'Black or White but never neutral: How readers perceive identity from yellow or skin-toned emoji'.

Chapter 8
- Doyle, Nancy (2020). Neurodiversity at Work.
- ADHD (Attention Deficit Hyperactivity Disorder)
- The National Institute of Health and Care Excellence https://cks.nice.org.uk/topics/attention-deficit-hyperactivity-disorder/background-information/
- Katzman, Martin; Bilkey, Timothy; Chokka, Pratap; Fallu, Angelo; and Klassen, Larry (2017). 'Adult ADHD and comorbid disorders: clinical implications of a dimensional approach'.
- DuPaul, George; Gormley, Matthew; and Laracy, Seth (2013). 'Comorbidity of LD and ADHD: implications of DSM-5 for assessment and treatment'.
- Willcutt, Eric and Pennington, Bruce (2000). 'Comorbidity of reading disability and attention-deficit/hyperactivity disorder: differences by gender and subtype'.

- Davis, Naomi and Kollins, Scott (2012). 'Treatment for co-occurring attention deficit/hyperactivity disorder and autism spectrum disorder'.

Dyslexia
- The British Dyslexia Association. https://www.bdadyslexia.org.uk/
- The British Dyslexic Association. 'Dyslexia Friendly Style Guide'. https://www.bdadyslexia.org.uk/advice/employers/creating-a-dyslexia-friendly-workplace/dyslexia-friendly-style-guide

Autism
- Mencap. 'Autism'. https://www.mencap.org.uk/learning-disability-explained/learning-disability-and-conditions/autism-asd
- The National Autistic Society. 'What is autism?' https://www.autism.org.uk/advice-and-guidance/what-is-autism
- The British Medical Association. 'Autism spectrum disorder'. https://www.bma.org.uk/what-we-do/population-health/improving-the-health-of-specific-groups/autism-spectrum-disorder

Chapter 9
- Adult Psychiatric Morbidity Survey (2014). https://digital.nhs.uk/data-and-information/publications/statistical/adult-psychiatric-morbidity-survey/adult-psychiatric-morbidity-survey-survey-of-mental-health-and-wellbeing-england-2014
- National Institute for Health and Care Excellence https://cks.nice.org.uk/topics/bipolar-disorder/background-information/incidence-prevalence
- Office for National Statistics Disability, 2019.
- Cree, Robyn A; Okoro, Catherine A; Zack, Matthew M; Carbone, Eric 2018. Frequent Mental Distress Among Adults, by Disability Status, Disability Type, and Selected Characteristics. https://pubmed.ncbi.nlm.nih.gov/32914770/

- Centers for Disease Control and Prevention (2018). 'Frequent Mental Distress Among Adults, by Disability Status, Disability Type, and Selected Characteristics – United States, 2018'.
- Wang, Ziyi, et al. (2021). 'Mapping global prevalence of depression among postpartum women'. https://www.nature.com/articles/s41398-021-01663-6
- Office for Health Improvement and Disparities. 'Adult substance misuse treatment statistics 2021 to 2022: report'. https://www.gov.uk/government/statistics/substance-misuse-treatment-for-adults-statistics-2021-to-2022/adult-substance-misuse-treatment-statistics-2021-to-2022-report
- Center for Behavioral Health Statistics and Quality (2017). 'National Survey on Drug Use and Health'.
- Stonewall and YouGov (2018). 'LGBT in Britain – Health (2018)'.
- GOV.UK. 'Detentions under the Mental Health Act'. https://www.ethnicity-facts-figures.service.gov.uk/health/mental-health/detentions-under-the-mental-health-act/latest/
- Barnett, Phoebe, et al. (2019). 'Ethnic variations in compulsory detention under the Mental Health Act: a systematic review and meta-analysis of international data'.

Chapter 10
- The Stroke Association. 'Aphasia and its effects'. https://www.stroke.org.uk/what-is-aphasia/aphasia-and-its-effects
- National Aphasia Association. https://aphasia.org/aphasia-resources/aphasia-statistics/
- Kauhanen, ML, et al. (2000). 'Aphasia, depression, and non-verbal cognitive impairment in ischaemic stroke'.

- Herbert, Ruth; Gregory, Emma; and Haw, Caroline (2018). 'Collaborative design of accessible information with people with aphasia'.

Chapter 11
- Sense. 'Deafblindness statistics in the UK'. https://www.sense.org.uk/about-us/statistics/deafblindness-statistics-in-the-uk/
- Portlock, Zoe. 'A guide to using subtitles, captions and transcripts for accessibility'. https://business.scope.org.uk/article/subtitles-closed-captions-transcripts-and-accessibility

Workshop - Naming things
- Downe, Lou. 'Good Services – How to design services that work'.
- GOV.UK. 'Naming your service'. https://www.gov.uk/service-manual/design/naming-your-service
- Design in government blog (2015). 'Good services are verbs, bad services are nouns'. https://designnotes.blog.gov.uk/2015/06/22/good-services-are-verbs-2/

A note about research

The aim of the research was to provide perspectives of people with a range of accessibility needs and describe how the tools, innovation, and their situational context affects how they experience digital content.

The method used was purposive sampling of a selection of participants, whose case studies act as the foundation for the inductive explorations and ideas in Parts 2 and 3. The technique for collecting the data I needed from each case study was to plan and undertake remote one-on-one contextual and generative interviews. Each interview was scheduled for 1 hour.

About the author

Rebekah Barry

Rebekah completed an undergraduate degree in English and a postgraduate in law. She worked with charities on family law and welfare benefits advice before joining the first user-centred design team at the UK-wide Citizens Advice.

User-centred design has remained the focus of Rebekah's work, and she continues to work with large public sector organisations, charities, and not for profits as a consultant.

Rebekah lives in Sussex with her partner, son, and cat.

I appreciate you

The biggest thank you goes to all the people who spoke to me about their lives and their experiences. Some of those conversations are included as case studies. I am forever grateful for your time and candour.

I have been massively fortunate to work with excellent, talented people over the years who have taught me everything. A few of those people are...

Sarah Winters, also known as my fairy godmother. Sarah gave me my first job in content design and entrusted me to write this book. Sarah phoned me about this embryonic book when I was a sleep-deprived, postpartum mess in the midst of an identity crisis. She had no idea that her fairy godmother's wand was offering not just a publishing contract but some professional purpose. Thank you, Sarah.

The first user-centred design team at Citizens Advice. Especially the welfare benefits crew. I learned so much from you all. Jo Hamilton Watson (research), Hannah Horton and Natalie Shaw (content), and Eliot Hill (design), among many others. I definitely struck gold there.

The DWP user-centred design team of old, expertly led by the complementary skills of Melanie Cannon and Ben Holliday. Huge thanks in particular to Tom Morgan, my partner in health assessment-related crime (take that sentence as you will). There couldn't have been a better group of people to work with on something so challenging. Bunch of superstars.

The thing all of these people have in common is that they'd probably all say they were just doing their job.

And for all help with the book...

Andrew Wiggan, for helping me with all the aspects of research and for saying, 'Did you make those changes yet?' a lot.

Alex Hall and Joanne Schofield, thank you for your brilliant questions and suggestions.

Dr. Anna Caute, for your expertise on aphasia and for being so helpful with contacts.

Rob Mills, this book would have had no structure without your help.

Rachel Edwards, for helping me with the final edits. Thank you for putting up with my 'perfect is the enemy of done' attitude (turns out that doesn't really work for books).

Craig Abbott, for the brilliant foreword, thoughtful suggestions, and the very timely encouragement that I needed.

Sarah Sheerman-Chase, for keeping me on track, always with kindness.

My mum and dad for the grandparenting duties, and literally everything else.